The
Guideposts
Christmas Celebration

The Editors of Guideposts

Phoenix Press

WALKER AND COMPANY
New York

The publisher wishes to thank *Tom Carey,* who worked so hard assembling this collection. We wish him well in his quest to become a priest.

First Published in the United States of America in 1987 by the Walker Publishing Company, Inc.

Published simultaneously in Canada by Thomas Allen & Son Canada, Limited, Markham, Ontario.

Printed in the United States of America

First Large Print Edition, 1987

See page 122 for Credits.

Library of Congress Cataloging-in-Publication Data

The Guideposts Christmas celebration.

   1. Christmas—Meditations. 2. Christmas—
Literary collections. I. Guideposts (Pawling, N.Y.)
BV45.G68   1987   242'.33   87-7937
ISBN 0-8028-2590-2 (lg. print)

Table of Contents

The
Guideposts
Christmas Celebration

PART I
Advent–
Preparing for Christmas

THE GREATEST STORY EVER TOLD

And Joseph also went up from Galilee, out of the city of Nazareth, into Judaea, unto the city of David, which is called Bethlehem . . . to be taxed with Mary his espoused wife, being great with child.

And so it was, that, while they were there, the days were accomplished that she should be delivered.

And she brought forth her firstborn Son, and wrapped Him in swaddling clothes, and laid Him in a manger; because there was no room for them in the inn.

And there were in the same country shepherds abiding in the field, keeping watch over their flock by night.

And, lo, the angel of the Lord came upon them, and the glory of the Lord shone round about them: and they were sore afraid.

And the angel said unto them, Fear not: for, behold, I bring you good tidings of great joy, which shall be to all people.

For unto you is born this day in the city of David a Saviour, which is Christ the Lord.

And this shall be a sign unto you; Ye shall find the Babe wrapped in swaddling clothes, lying in a manger.

And suddenly there was with the angel a multitude of the heavenly host praising God, and saying, Glory to God in the highest, and on earth peace, goodwill toward men.

LUKE 2:4-14

A CHRISTMAS SAMPLER BOX

Ruth C. Ikerman

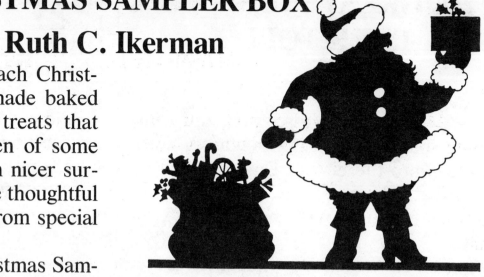

One of the joys of each Christmas season is all the home-made baked goodies and mouth-watering treats that come popping out of the oven of some creative homemaker. An even nicer surprise at Christmas is to receive thoughtful gifts of home-baked goodies from special friends.

Have you thought of a Christmas Sampler Box of seasonal treats with a little bit of this, and a little bit of that, to share with trusty friends? You don't have to pack a whole loaf of nut bread. Put two or three slices in a waxed sandwich bag, then wrap it in foil, and place it in that empty box which formerly held the cards you've now addressed and sent.

Next to the foil-covered sack, put three or four of your favorite sugar cookies covered with red and green sprinkles. Then add a piece of brown sugar fudge with a big half-walnut on top, or a piece of white divinity covered with coconut. Or try some candied orange peel or grapefruit peel.

These small seasonal treats add up to large quantities of pleasure and happiness for the receiver. They can be sent through the mail also. In fact, one of the most appreciated gifts I made one year was a dozen fruit cookies, mailed to an elderly couple in another state.

They wrote: "We are slower now in getting out our cards, and the sight of these lovely cookies somehow persuades us to keep on writing personal notes. It saved us a trip to the store, too, for it was a cold day and we didn't really want to go outside."

My gesture had been such a simple thing to do, but the results were rewarding. Why not try giving a Christmas Sampler Box this season to those who long to remember the fragrance of a home kitchen?

THE RED MITTENS

Rosalyn Hart Finch

Christmas was coming and I was doing some heavy complaining to Mama about pocket money. "All the other kids in fifth grade are gonna **buy** their Christmas gifts," I said pointedly, when Mama suggested that "home-made gifts are more love-filled than **bought** ones."

"How come we always have to be poor?" I grumbled.

"Being poor has nothing to do with giving," said Mama. "It's not what you give, but **how** you give."

But I didn't agree.

Christmas week was unseasonably warm for Ohio, turning the month-long layers of snow into messy puddles and slush. But things began looking up for me; I had an idea.

Early on Saturday morning I bundled up my five-year-old brother, Dicky, who owned the one and only wagon on the block, jammed my way into my mackinaw, shoved on boots and gloves, emptied the wagon of Dicky's junk, and took off with Dicky in it.

Across the backyard and through the stubbled cornfield that edged along the rear of our property and spread as far as our eyes could see, I trotted, pulling Dicky and the wagon behind me. The wagon wheels fitted neatly in between the rows of stubble, but pulling Dicky through the half-thawed slush was rough. I was so fired up with enthusiasm for my plan, however, that I scarcely noticed.

At last, reaching the train tracks bordering the cornfield, I unfolded my plan to Dicky.

"What we're gonna do, Dicky, is load the wagon with all the hunks of coal we can find beside the tracks. Then we'll take it to the gas station and sell it. A girl in my class says her cousin does it all the time. We're lucky the snow's mostly melted or we couldn't see it."

"For money?" Dicky's eyes widened. "Will I get some, too?"

"Sure," I promised. "We both will."

"Oh, boy." Dicky scuttled out of the wagon, eager to begin. "How'd this stuff get here?" he asked, stooping to brush the remaining slush from a chunk of "black gold."

"It falls off the trains," I cried happily, tossing chunks into the wagon as fast as I could pick them up. I'd never dreamed there'd be so much.

In short order we had stacked a small black mountain and were headed toward the gas station, Dicky pushing and me pulling. By the time we'd reached the road to the station, Dicky was whining and crying, filled with cold and fatigue.

An old woman I'd often seen at church, Mrs. Scott, was out sweeping the slush from her front porch. "What's wrong, children?" she called.

"Nothing," I yelled back. "My brother's just cold."

"Why don't you bring him inside by the stove? I could fix you both some hot cocoa."

Dicky ran to the offered haven. Much as I'd have loved a little warmth and some cocoa, I declined. I was anxious to get the money the coal would bring me. I left Dicky and said I'd be back.

Puffing and blowing, I trudged the lead-heavy load the rest of the way alone. My numb feet were stumbling at everything and my fingers burned. My heart hit bottom when the gas station man said, "Didn't cha' notice the weather's turned? We ain't buyin' any more coal. We're full up."

Tears of disappointment stung my eyes and lumped my throat. I hastily fled the warmth of the station's little stove, grabbed the wagon handle and ran back, tears streaming down my face. How I arrived at Mrs. Scott's house again I don't recall.

"Dicky has to go home now," I managed to say looking down at the ground.

"Whatever's the matter, dear?" Mrs. Scott said, drawing me gently inside and wiping my tear-stained face with her apron. "Come by the kitchen stove for some cocoa."

Dicky pulled my sleeve. "Didja get the money? Didja get the money?" he jabbered, holding out a ready hand.

That did it. My misery broke loose and I sobbed out my disappointment. "There isn't any money. The gas station man wouldn't buy the coal."

Dicky hugged my knees in silent commiseration.

When I lifted my head to wipe my tears, Mrs. Scott held out a steaming cup

cupboard, reached up to the top shelf and lifted down an ancient yellowing teapot. Pulling off the lid, she dumped out a dollar bill, a dime and a nickle.

"Would this be enough to buy your coal?" she asked, spreading it out on the table.

Money! My eyes fairly leapt at the sight of it there, then lingered on Mrs. Scott's hands as they smoothed out the dollar bill. They were red and rough. I raised my eyes and for the first time noticed the patch on her apron and the faded kitchen curtains and the newspaper taped to the windows.

My heart sank. **She couldn't really spare the money for the coal.**

A pile of bright red mittens sat on the countertop. I looked at them curiously. "I just knitted those for our missionary society," she said. "Here, try a pair." They were much too big for me, but I didn't let on.

"They're beautiful," I said, for they were. "I bet anyone would love to have them." Staring at the money on the table I suddenly knew what to say. "I'll trade you the coal for a pair of mittens, Mrs. Scott."

"Would you really like them?" asked

of cocoa. "What a shame, dear. Dicky told me how hard you both worked."

I nodded. "I was counting on it for a Christmas present for my class exchange."

Mrs. Scott kept shaking her head, clucking sympathetically. Then her concerned face brightened.

"Say, you know I could use that coal myself," she said. She hurried over to the

Mrs. Scott. I nodded.

"I think we've made a fine exchange," she beamed as she pulled her sweater about her shoulders. It was chilly away from the stove. . . .

Well, I ended up giving one of Mama's "homemade gifts" for my class gift-exchange that year, and I kept Mrs. Scott's snug red mittens for myself. Her gift warmed my hands all winter long and more importantly, my heart was warmed whenever I thought of my gift of coal to her.

Mama was right. Love-filled gifts are the best. Mrs. Scott and I had made a fine exchange.

MAKE A LITTLE MANGER

There was no room in the inn
   For me,
Will you make a little manger
   In your heart?
Into this warm and lighted haven
   Will you bring Someone cold,
And lonely, and friendless?
   Thus love will be born again
Beneath the star!

BARBARA GOODEN

"FOR-THE-BIRDS" CHRISTMAS

May Sheridan Gold

It started off as a miserable Advent. All three children were confined to the house with the flu and I didn't know how to perk up their sad little spirits as Christmas approached. They were getting bored and restless. I had my hands full with shopping, decorating and baking, with very little time left over to entertain them.

One morning I found them crouched in the dining room staring at something outside the floor-length window. I tiptoed behind them to catch a glimpse of what was occupying their attention, when they jumped up and pulled me down to their level.

"Look, Mother," Elizabeth, the youngest, cried. "See the red birds and the sparrows hopping around on the snow? They're probably hungry and don't know where to get food." I watched in fascination as the tiny creatures bobbed up and down, fluttering in the snow and around the majestic evergreen which adorned a corner of our yard.

"Couldn't we do something?" Andy, my ten-year-old pleaded.

"Yeah," Skip, eight, agreed, "maybe we could put some plates of bread crumbs outside."

"No," said Andy, "the cats will get them. Can't we put them on the evergreen?" Three round faces looked eagerly at me for approval.

"I think that's a wonderful idea, children," I said, proud of their concern for the poor birds. "Let's go in the kitchen and see what we can come up with." The three eager beavers trotted behind me, and for the next hour we were on a scavenger hunt in the kitchen: popcorn, cranberries, sunflower seeds, raisins, apples, even peanut butter—the children were very inventive!

For the next few days and evenings, trimming the tree for the birds became our family project. Hours were spent making the decorations, and each evening my husband Dan or I went outside and hung them on the evergreen tree—some on strings and some attached with pipe cleaners. The children were so busy and excited, they soon forgot their confinement and were back in good health before Christmas arrived.

Now, each Christmas at our house is "for-the-birds," as well as for our family. Maybe you'd like to start this family tradition at your house. Here are some of the items we've used:

Strings of popcorn

Strings of cranberries

Old jar tops: Spread each with a mixture of peanut butter and 1 Tbs. or more of corn meal; or spread with cold bacon fat. Press into these mixtures: sunflower seeds, raisins, cranberries, other bird seed.

Coffee can tops: Again, spread with peanut butter mixture, and with cranberries or raisins form a star design on the peanut butter. (Birds love peanut butter, especially in winter.)

Apples: Put toothpicks on all sides of apple (porcupine style). On the tip of each pick, place a raisin or cranberry.

Tips on attracting birds to your tree: Put sunflower seeds or bird seed on ground around tree or in aluminum pie pan at base of tree, but out where it can be seen by birds. Especially after a fresh snowfall, put seeds around tree to help guide the birds to the treats you've provided.

IN THE BLEAK MID-WINTER

In the bleak mid-winter, frosty wind
    made moan,
Earth stood hard as iron, water like a
    stone,
Snow had fallen, snow on snow, snow on
    snow,
In the bleak mid-winter, long ago.

What can I give Him, poor as I am?
If I were a shepherd, I would bring a
    lamb;
If I were a Wise Man, I would do my
    part;
Yet what can I give Him? I will give my
    heart.

CHRISTMAS FINGER PRINTS

June Masters Bacher

You can—you **do**—own your own private "printing" press!

This year why don't you and your family—all ages—design your own original greeting cards for the holidays? They will be different from anybody else's because no two sets of finger prints are exactly the same. And that is what you will be using.

First, choose any kind of white or colored paper you wish to use. You will also need a felt-tip-pen and an ink pad. And, of course, your nonidentical printing press.

Just place your thumb or finger on the ink pad—hard. Then press the inked finger on the paper, rolling just a little from left to right. Continue adding prints until you have created a design—a Christmas Tree, a cross, an animal, a star, a shepherd—there's no end to the holiday pictures you can create with your finger prints.

Use the felt-tipped pen to outline your design and add such touches as a crook for the shepherd, lights on the Christmas tree, streams of light from the star. Let your imagination run wild and your friends will know immediately they are receiving something very special this Christmas. And for you and your family it can be a warm memory of another Christmas shared.

QUIETNESS

May the quietness of Christmas,
The calm and holy hush
Of that first advent season,
Still our Christmas rush.

May our memories of the manger
Reassure us, and ease the stress
Of troubled hearts in troubled times
With His peace and quietness. Amen

KAY L. HALLIWILL

THE BLESSING OF THE CRÈCHE

Sue Monk Kidd

One Christmas I traveled to Bethlehem. There is a little shop there that sits on a winding road, not far from the nativity cave. As I stepped inside, a dark-eyed man with a wide, white smile appeared at my elbow. "May I help you, Madam?" he said with a nicely polished Hebrew accent.

"I'm looking for a creche," I replied. "A nativity set."

His eyes gleamed like two black pearls. He made a little bow to the rear of the store. I followed him along an aisle until suddenly he stepped aside, sweeping out his arm, and there in the middle of a table sat a creche. A creche so splendid it seemed to glow with the ancient holiness that inspired it. It had been carved from the olive trees that dotted the Judean hills like green umbrellas. The rich wood shone warm and golden in the dim light of the little shop. I touched each piece with reverence. Only moments before I had stood in the heart of the holy cave where Jesus was born and my heart was still full.

The salesman stood nearby like a bird on a perch, his shoulders curved forward, his eyes darting. "You like, Madam?" he asked, as my fingers touched the tiny tips of the star carved atop the stable.

He stepped closer. "It is the finest wood. And the workmanship is unmatched," he said. I nodded.

I walked around the table, trying to make up my mind. "I'm not sure," I said.

"Ah, but Madam, you must have it!" he said. "A Bethlehem creche has secret blessings!"

In the end I purchased the creche, not for its alleged "secret blessings," but because of its irresistible beauty and because I was in Bethlehem and the long-ago miracle still lived in the air.

I stored it in a cardboard box in the attic. The next Christmas, I wanted to make the creche's first appearance beneath our tree special. I thought and wondered. How could it touch my family with the Bethlehem miracle? I found myself remembering the words of the salesman, "A Bethlehem creche has secret blessings." Perhaps he was right. Perhaps God **could** bless and inspire our lives through its presence, if only we let Him. And not just with a Bethlehem creche . . . but **any** creche, even the tiny one my daughter had made from popsicle sticks one Christmas past.

So I sat down and wrote a prayer. Then, filled with anticipation, I climbed to the attic and brought down the cardboard box. That night, with the tree lights shining in the darkness and dancing on the windows, my family gathered around the tree. An almost reverent silence settled about us as softly as a whisper in church. My husband opened the lid. The children took turns standing each item of the creche beneath the tree as I read my prayer aloud:

It is time, Lord. Time to take the holy drama from this cardboard box and set it beneath the tree. As I blow away the dust, may this little creche come to life in our home and bestow its secret blessings.

Bless this wooden stable, Lord. This lowly abode of cows and donkeys. May it keep me humble this Christmas.

Bless this tiny star beaming at the top. May it light my eyes with the wonder of Your caring.

Bless the little angel. May her song flow through our house and fill it with smiles.

Bless this caring shepherd and the small lamb cradled in his arms. May it whisper of Your caring embrace on my life.

Bless these Wise Men bearing splendid gifts. May they inspire me to lay my shining best at Your feet.

Bless this earthly father in his simple robe. May he remind me of all You have entrusted to my care.

Bless this Virgin Mother. May she teach me patience as I tend to my own little ones.

And bless this Baby nestled in the hay. May the love He brought to earth that Bethlehem night so fill my heart with compassion and warmth that it becomes a Christmas gift to those around me.

Now the creche is here, Lord . . . and we are holy participants in Your miracle night.

May Your secret blessings come to us as a spark from Your glory . . . a candle that never goes out.

Amen.

I can't tell you **exactly** what happened to us that night, but I do know that I experienced a special holiness and a reverence for our family that stayed with me all through the Christmas season. That was my "secret blessing," and perhaps each of us shared the same "secret." For this little ritual has become the single most important Christmas preparation for our family.

TO A FRIEND AT CHRISTMAS

He knew we needed someone
   to share each happy day.
To be a source of courage
   when troubles come our way.
Someone who is true to us
   together or apart,
Someone whose love we'll always
   hold
   and treasure in our hearts.

ANTHONY GUAGENTI

SO REMEMBER . . .

So remember while December
Brings the only Christmas day,
In the year let there be Christmas
In the things you do and say;
Wouldn't life be worth the living
Wouldn't dreams be coming true
If we kept the Christmas spirit
All the whole year through?

ANONYMOUS

GRANDMOTHER'S CHRISTMAS ANGEL

Marilyn Morgan Helleberg

Like most kids, I heard lots of warnings, in December, about being good because Santa was coming, but Grandmother didn't talk about Santa much. Instead, she used to tell us about a beautiful angel named Amiah, who went around every year, just before Christmas, looking for the perfect birthplace for the Baby Jesus.

Amiah wasn't looking for a palace or a church or even a manger. She was looking for a warm and loving human heart. Grandmother said **that** was the perfect birthplace for God's Son. Then she'd as if we knew of any hearts that might be available. I can remember trying especially hard to be loving, as Christmas drew near, in the hope that **my** heart might be picked. I guess I didn't realize then, that Jesus could be born in millions of hearts at the same time.

Still, about this time every year, I think about Amiah, and I seem to hear Grandmother's voice saying "Is your heart warm and loving enough to be chosen as the birthplace of Jesus **this** year?

"MOTHER HELPED ME DO IT"

Drue Duke

The pungent fragrance of the decorated pine tree filled the house, hanging especially heavy in the kitchen's warm air. Soon the fruitcake I had put into the oven would add its spicy smell.

I slipped the mixing bowl and measuring cup into the dishwasher and checked my list on the counter.

"Cheese straws next," I said aloud.

I had a lot to do in preparing for our annual Christmas open house. But the last thing I needed in my compact kitchen was a pair of eighty-five-year-old hands.

Yet, there she was, at my elbow, asking her persistent question, "What can I do to help you?"

I felt my jaw tighten against the words I didn't want to say. Mother knew that we were delighted to have her come for a visit over Christmas with us. She knew, too, of my long-standing determination that she would do no work while in my home. One of God's basic commandments is to honor one's father and mother, and there was no greater dishonor I could do her than to shove my chores off on her.

"Why don't you go into the den and enjoy television?" I managed to ask patiently.

"There's nothing good on now." She leaned against a base cabinet, exactly where I needed to get. "It's some story I don't understand."

I knew she had difficulty hearing at times and couldn't always unravel the plots on TV. And since she was alone all day while I was at work, she probably was lonesome to be with me. A quick surge of love and tenderness for her made me say gently, "I'll pull a dining room chair out here and you can sit and talk to me. How's that?"

From the chair that I placed out of my

way she watched me line up ingredients along the counter.

"I'll grate the cheese for you," she volunteered brightly.

"Now, Mother, that arthritis in your hands . . ."

"Honey!" she cut in so sharply I turned to look at her. "This arthritis," holding up a wrinkled hand, "doesn't hurt nearly so badly as just being useless."

"Oh, Mother!" The hunk of cheese banged on the counter as I let it go to slip an arm about her. "You are not useless!"

"I may be old," she said stoutly, "but there are some things I can still do."

"Of course there are." I turned back to the counter, clearing a place. "Such as grating cheese. Right?"

We smiled at each other and she stood up, ready to get busy. I put a high stool up to the counter. She could not get up on the seat, but she propped against it long enough to grate the cheese. While she worked, she chatted brightly about two sisters who always brought cheese straws to the senior citizens' meetings, back home in Georgia.

"I think I'll sit down a bit," she said when the cheese was a mound of golden shreds.

From the corner of my eye I could see her hands shaking. I knew she was tired, but her flushed face was beaming. Her talking had caused me to forget how much flour I had measured, and I had to redo it.

But as I measured, I realized there was something far more wrong than my need to redo—it was my attitude. How foolish I had been! I brought her into my home, but had not made her a part of it. I had treated her like an ornament that was nice but not necessary. I called my actions "honoring" when in reality they were hurting. I hadn't looked closely enough to see her need to be needed.

"I plan to do the salted nuts tomorrow night," I said in a quick decision. "But I haven't shelled the pecans. If I crack them tonight, will you pick them out for me tomorrow?"

"Of course I will." She rocked forward on the chair, stretching toward me. "Anything I can do to help you, just tell me."

My mind searched and found another request.

"You know that arrangement with the red candles that I made for the mantle," I asked. "I'm not satisfied with it. I wish you would help me remake it."

As my hands moved through the heavy dough, mixing flour and water and cheese, she watched and made small talk. A smile played about her lips, and I realized I was wearing one to match it. It was a precious moment for both of us, one I knew how to keep.

In days to come I'd ask her to fold some towels from the dryer, to stamp envelopes for Christmas cards, to lay out silver on the party table—all tasks she could handle. If the results were less than perfect, what difference would it make?

And when our guests commented on a lovely party, how proud we both would be that I could say, "Mother helped me do it!"

THE ADVENT COOKIE TREE

Sue Monk Kidd

On December 1st I pull out the sugar cookie recipe that my Mama has used for thirty-one Christmases. My mind remembers back to the cookie tree tradition she began when I was a small child. Every Christmas her treasured sugar cookies dangled from a five-tiered wooden tree my father made. Now the cookie tree has come to live at my house. But we have combined Mama's tradition with our own special observance of Advent.

The children drag stools over to the kitchen counter to stand on; I tie on an apron and the cookie baking begins. After the dough is rolled out, we set out twenty-four special cookie cutters . . . a star, a donkey, an angel, a wreath, a manger, etc. Each has its own meaning in the coming of Christ. The children take turns cutting out the shapes, two of each one in case one breaks. Then we bake them, and later decorate them with icing and store them in an airtight container.

Each night the family gathers around the cookie tree and one cookie is hung on the tree till Christmas. We talk about each shape as it finds a place upon the branches. I tell them the wreath-shaped cookie stands for the unending circle of God's love . . . the donkey for the humility of Christ's coming . . . the star for God's guiding light. Sometimes we sing an appropriate song, like "Away in a Manger," the night the manger is hung.

The children count away the days till Christmas by watching the cookies grow to the top of the tree. But more importantly, we all share together the meaning of Christ's coming in an enchanting way that my children are not likely to forget.

WHY CHRISTMAS TREES ARE NOT PERFECT

Dick Schneider

They say that if you creep into an evergreen forest late at night you can hear the trees talking. In the whisper of the wind you'll catch the older pines reassuring the younger ones why they'll never be perfectly shaped.

There will always be a bent branch here, a gap there . . .

Long, long ago evergreens **were** perfect, with each taking pride in branches sloping evenly from crown to symmetrical skirt.

This was particularly true in a small kingdom deep in Europe beyond the Carpathian Mountains.

On the first Saturday of Advent the Queen's woodsmen would search the royal evergreen forest for the most perfect tree. It would then reign in honor in the great castle hall, shimmering with silver balls and golden angels that sparkled in the light of thousands of candles. While a huge Yule log chuckled and crackled, the royal family and villagers together would dance and sing around the tree in celebration.

Out in the hushed forest every evergreen vied for this honor, each endeavoring to grow their branches and needles to perfection. They strained at the task, fully concentrating on their form and appearance.

One cold night when a bright white moon glittered on the crusty snow as if it were strewn with millions of diamonds, a small rabbit limped into a grove of evergreens, its sides heaving in panic. Beyond the hill rose the yelping of village dogs in the thrill of the hunt.

The rabbit, eyes wide with fright, frantically searched for cover, but found nothing among the dark trunks extending upwards into branches artfully lifted from the snow.

Faster and faster the cottontail circled as the excited yelping sounded louder and louder. The trees looked askance at this interruption of their evening (when growing was at its best).

And then a small pine shuddered. Of all the young trees, it had the promise of being the finest of the forest. Everything about it, from its deep sea-green color to the delicate curl of its branches, was perfect.

But now . . . its lower branches began to dip, down, down to the ground. And in that instant before the slavering dogs broke into the clearing, the rabbit found safety within the evergreen screen. In the morning the bunny found its burrow. But the little pine could not quite lift its branches. No matter; perhaps a little irregularity in a tree so beautiful would not be noticed.

Then a powerful blizzard lashed the land. The villagers slammed shutters closed while birds and animals huddled in nests and dens. A small wren, blown astray, desperately sought sanctuary in the evergreens. But each one she approached clenched its branches tight like a fist.

Finally, in exhaustion, she fell into the little pine. The pine's heart opened and so did its branches, and the wren slept within them, warm and secure. But the pine had difficulty rearranging its branches. There would be a gap, evermore.

Weeks passed and winter deepened, bringing a gale such as never before experienced in the mountains. It caught a small fawn that had wandered from its mother. Head down, blinded by snow, it inched into the evergreens, seeking a windbreak. But the trees held their branches open so the wind could whistle through them and avoid dangerous bending or breaking of their limbs.

Again the little pine took pity and now tightly closed its branches forming an impenetrable wall behind which the fawn huddled out of the gale. But alas, when the wind ceased, the small pine had been severely and permanently bent out of shape.

A tear of pine gum oozed from a branch tip. Now it could never hope for the honor it had longed for since it was a seedling.

Lost in despair, the little pine did not see the good Queen come into the forest. She had come to choose the finest tree herself.

As her royal sleigh slowly passed through the forest her practiced eye scanned the evergreens now preening themselves. When she saw the little pine, a flush of anger filled her. What right had a tree with such defects to be in the royal forest? Reminding herself to have a woodsman dispose of it, she drove on, but then stopped and glanced back at it. As she gazed on it, she noticed the tracks of small animals that had found shelter under it and a downy feather within its branches where a bird had rested. And, as she studied the gaping hole in its side and its wind-whipped trunk, understanding filled her heart.

"This one," she said. Her attendants gasped. And to the astonishment of the forest, the little pine was borne to the great hall. And everyone who danced and sang around it said it was the finest Christmas tree yet. For in looking at its gnarled and worn branches, many saw the protecting arm of their father, others the comforting bosom of a mother, and some, as did the wise Queen, saw the love of Christ expressed on earth.

So if you walk among evergreens today, you will find, along with rabbits, birds and other happy living things, drooped branches providing cover, gaps offering resting places, forms bent from wrestling winter winds.

For, as with many of us, the trees have learned that the scars suffered for the sake of others makes one most beautiful in the eyes of God. ▲

THE MESSAGE FROM THE MANGER

May the fragrance of the season
wreathe round your heart today;
May you find a tiny margin
of time when you can pray.
Let the message from the manger
bless you, lead you, guide you
    still;
Join the choir of heavenly angels,
sing "Peace on earth . . . Good
    will."

June Masters Bacher

THE UGLY OLD TABLE

Elizabeth Sherrill

The table wasn't really very attractive to begin with, with its imitation-wood Formica top and spindly wrought iron legs, the kind of furniture you buy when the children are young. For the last twelve years, what's worse, it's been badly scarred—a great circular scorch mark right in the center of it. We've got to get rid of it, and yet . . .

I know the scar is twelve years old because it was twelve years ago that Scott, the oldest of our three children, went away to college. Now he was home for Christmas vacation. I remember that I baked a ham (his favorite) the Sunday he arrived, and of course I made the yam casserole that's as traditional with us as the lights on the tree.

Before sitting down, we lit the Advent wreath in the center of the table. It was at its brightest this fourth Sunday of Advent, all four purple candles lit, each a measure of the passing of time toward the long-awaited birth of the Saviour: the first now a mere nub, the fourth still tall and new.

For a while we gazed at them in their homemade wooden holder surrounded with hemlock twigs Donn had brought from the woods. **The Light of the world is drawing very close,** said the dancing flames. Then we turned our attention to the food and the catching up we had to do.

We'd been at the table an hour when Liz jumped up. "My show! It's on!"

I hurried after her to the TV room. The program was one her ballet teacher had urged her to see—the Christmas story told in dance by a black troupe from

26

Harlem.

It was a shame for the male members of the family to miss it, in spite of their oft-repeated views on dance in all its forms.

"You've got to see this!" I called. "Hurry!"

So in they came, John wearing his fatherly-duty smile, Scott and Donn exchanging suffering-brother looks. But "Black Madonna" really **was** exciting. I could tell by the way the three of them, in spite of themselves, were soon leaning forward, totally engrossed.

Until Donn glanced up. "I smell something," he said.

Then we all did. We dashed to the kitchen. Nothing there. "The dining room!" said Scott. He shoved open the door and clouds of smoke engulfed us. "The table's on fire!"

Frantically we snatched up bowls, pots, whatever was closest. We filled them at the sink and rushed to the dining room, bumping into each other until we established a kind of bucket-brigade order.

Later, opening windows to clear out the smoke, we reconstructed what had happened.

Unpardonably, we'd left the room with the candles still burning. The shortest one must have reached the hemlock needles almost at once. The blaze had been so hot it had bubbled the Formica.

As we scraped as the mess of ashes, water and melted wax, the "what-if" struck us. What if we'd replaced this old table as we'd meant to do for years, and gotten the walnut one my heart was set on? If the wreath had been on a wooden table there was no doubt in any of our minds that the whole room, and probably the house, would have been on fire before we reached it. We were down to the surface of the table. The only damage was that circular burn scar.

The "if" hadn't happened. Instead we'd been protected, one more time, from our own stupidity. It was as though God had foreseen our thoughtless behavior and, without our knowing or deserving, prepared the way out ahead of time.

And wasn't that, we asked ourselves, in its own way a symbol of Advent? Wasn't this what happened at this season, each year? Even before we are aware of our peril, was God silently, surely, preparing our Redemption, which is born at Christmas?

As I say, it's really an ugly old table. But somehow we keep hanging onto it.

LET CHRISTMAS HAPPEN TO YOU

DR. NORMAN VINCENT PEALE

Christmas is a season of joy and laughter when our cup of happiness brims over. Yet increasingly we hear negative remarks about what a burden the holiday season has become.

This indicates that something is wrong somewhere because Christ never meant His birthday to be anything but a glorious event. Christianity is designed for the transmission of power from Jesus Christ to the individual; a Christ-centered Christmas, therefore, should be the year's climactic experience.

Perhaps we need to use more imagination in recapturing this experience in a personal way, like some creative people are doing.

The members of one family, during a financial crisis, made personally, by hand, all Christmas gifts for each other. That particular Christmas was such a joyful one that its plan has been continued ever since.

A church congregation was asked to bring in all the old clothes they could spare for distribution to the needy. One family sent in all new clothes, bought with money diligently saved all year to buy each other Christmas presents.

Such giving surely expresses the true meaning of the birthday of Our Lord. We honor Him when we live the examples He set. An act of mercy that reflects the inspiration He gave us will create a deeper satisfaction than giving or receiving the most expensive gift.

The Psalmist says: "I will remember the works of the Lord: surely I will re-

member thy wonders of old."* The early Christians celebrated Christmas by remembering the works of the Lord and the wonders of old. It was a day for gaiety, but not for excesses. How many people do we know who make gift-giving a burden because they spend beyond their means?

Giving at Christmas can take many forms not measured by dollars. Here are a few simple suggestions for such giving:

A gift you make yourself is more appreciated—something as simple as a fruit cake or a letter opener; a surprise photo of a friend's house, babies or pets. A couple we know painted the porch and front door of their parents' house. To the giver it is a labor of love; to the receiver an offering of love.

Send Christmas remembrances to those who would least expect it from you, the people we often encounter but do not really know: the neighbor who nods good morning daily; the people who clean your office or workroom; the officer who directs traffic at your corner. Best of all, the one with whom you are most annoyed!

Making it a point to find out more about these people is an enriching experience. Get the thrill of trips to a hospital, orphanage, a jail. Also it is a wonderful Christmas adventure to help the families of such unfortunates.

Often it is left to children to show us the way to a happier Christmas observance.

In a Western public school the sixth graders were told that in many other lands the religious expression of Christmas was much more important than gift giving. These lively youngsters were understandably surprised, and asked:

"How then should we celebrate the holiday?"

Their teacher asked them all to find the answer in the Bible. One boy wrote this answer:

"I was hungered, and ye gave me meat: I was thirsty, and ye gave me drink . . . As ye have done it unto the least of these my brethren ye have done it unto me . . ."**

That was a good beginning, the teacher told them, and suggested that they find the least of their brethren in their own town. They did, and collected their Christmas Fund in an empty jar.

On Christmas Day there was enough in the jar for Christmas dinners and gifts for two families. And the children themselves took their gifts to both families. On the way back one of the teachers saw a little girl tightly clutching the empty mayonnaise jar that had held the Christmas fund.

"I'm going to put it under my tree at home," the little girl explained all aglow, "to remind me of the loveliest Christmas I've ever had."

Let such a Christ-like Christmas happen to you. It will be your most glorious Christmas.

*PSALMS 77:11
**MATTHEW 25:35-40

PART II
The Joys of Christmas

"AND IT CAME TO PASS . . ."

And it came to pass in those days, that there went out a decree from Caesar Augustus, that all the world should be taxed. (And this taxing was first made when Cyrenius was governor of Syria.) And all went to be taxed, every one into his own city. And Joseph also went up from Galilee, out of the city of Nazareth, into Judaea, unto the city of David, which is called Bethlehem; (because he was of the house and lineage of David:) to be taxed with Mary his espoused wife, being great with child . . .

LUKE 2:1-5

GIFTS

Maxine Montgomery

I have heard critics negating the value of exchanging gifts at Christmas. It's a pagan custom, they say. Or, it's a scheme on the part of the merchandisers to make a fortune on our gullibility. In many cases, that may be right. But what is more beautiful than giving a much-needed, long-wanted gift to a dear one in the name of our Lord? Christmas is a time set apart to remember the miraculous birth of the Son of God; God's gift to humanity. The magi, astonished and deeply reverent, gave their fortunes to the Holy Child, and Joseph used that gift to take his Child into Egypt out of danger from Herod. So we who love the Lord seek to express our love to others by the giving of gifts. When a gift is given in the name of love and goodwill, it is a beautiful thing. It is the joyous privilege of Christians to use the goodwill and tenderness that is a part of Christmas to bring peace and joy into the hearts of those who do not know Christ!

THE TOUCH OF THE ANGEL'S WINGS

 ## Idella Bodie

It was Christmas Eve. Elizabeth sat on the edge of her little daughter's bed. She bent over and kissed the rose-petaled cheek. With golden-flax hair spreading over the pillow and long lashes heavy with sleep, Marya looked for all the world like an angel.

Elizabeth's heart swelled with love and overflowed with the sweet joy of sharing. On this, the holiest night, she had told her little daughter about the visit of the angel.

The two of them had sat listening to the delicate Swedish chimes and watching the little angels dance round and round above the glow of magical candles. The first Christmas after Marya was born, Elizabeth's mother had given her the family keepsake. "Because you always loved it so," her mother had said.

Earlier, as Elizabeth saw the glow of the candles reflected in her little daughter's blue eyes, she felt the tender excite-ment mounting until the two of them and the candles were one. And Elizabeth knew it was time to share her marvelous secret.

With joy swelling even greater Elizabeth remembered the first Christmas the angel had given her the joy of the Christmas season.

She was about Marya's age the evening she sat at the table long after the dishes had been cleared away. With her chin cupped in her hands, she followed the movement of the angels and the light tinkling of the chimes.

"Elizabeth is enchanted by those angel chimes," her mother announced to no one in particular.

It was that night Elizabeth was awakened by the soft **whir-r-r.**

Moonlight shimmered through the curtains of her bedroom window like the lace on her grandmother's dresses. Elizabeth

lay very still. Then in the soft darkness she saw the angel—one of them from the chimes—moving around her room. Moonlight frosted the tips of the angel's wings and the tiny horn at her mouth made the softest of sounds like twinkling bits of laughter.

Suddenly a silver magic enveloped the room, making Elizabeth's heart tremble. But she was not afraid. Under covers streaked by moonlight she marveled at the angel's fluttering. She saw the gossamer wings brush the dolls on the trunk against the wall, her dollhouse, the edges of her storybooks, her clothes. And with the touch the whole room became a place of heavenly sweetness.

And then as quietly as the enchantment had come, it disappeared. The whirring stopped and the angel was gone. Yet a glory shone over the room until Elizabeth fell asleep again.

The next morning, it was as if the angel's wings had cleansed and blessed the

world. How new everything looked! The faces of her dolls were clear and bright. Even the air smelled clean. It was as if Elizabeth was seeing and feeling everything for the first time. Her whole world was different—it had been touched by the angel's wings.

Eager to share, she had burst into the kitchen where her parents and brothers had already gathered around the breakfast table.

"Last night," she began, pointing to the little angels standing frozen in their angelic poses, "one of the angels came to my room and—"

"Yeah, Elizabeth—" Her brothers' laughter cut across her beautiful story.

"Boys!" her mother reprimanded. "Elizabeth has a vivid imagination." And Elizabeth thought she detected a trace of a smile at the corner of her father's mouth.

Even so, the angel's touch filled the Christmas season with wonder and magic.

On other Christmases the angel's coming was never quite the same. Once or twice she heard the whirring or the faint tooting of the horn. Another time she saw the moonlight frosting gossamer wings in flight. But Elizabeth knew the little angel always came and that the coming gave the world a special glow of miracles.

And tonight, after carrying this beautiful secret in her heart for all these years, she had shared it with her very own little girl. Now the beauty and magic of the angel's touch would live forever as it passed from heart to heart in love.

Those without faith might say it was just a dream, but Elizabeth knew that she had been chosen by God to be blessed with the gift of the angel's visit. For only those who believe can know the touch of the angel's wings and the miracles it brings. For in them Christ is born again each Christmas.

Perhaps tonight Marya would be awakened by the soft whir of wings.

EMMETT McCALLISTER'S CHRISTMAS EVE
An old Christmas tale retold

Kathryn Slattery

Emmett McCallister sighed restlessly as he poked at the smoldering remains of what had been a raging blaze in his fireplace. He debated whether or not to put on another log or turn out the lights and go to bed. It was Christmas Eve and his wife Martha had gone to midnight mass.

"Emmett," she had said softly while wrapping a woolen muffler tightly around her neck, "won't you consider coming with me? It's going to be a beautiful Christmas service—complete with carols and candles. I think you really might enjoy it."

"No, Martha," Emmett had replied, shaking his head stubbornly. "No church. No carols. No candles. You know how I feel about Christmas. I think it's a lot of hogwash." For a moment Emmett felt badly, noticing the pained look in Martha's eyes. But then he stiffened, determined not to let his emotions get the better of him.

"Now you be careful," he said gruffly, offering his wife a perfunctory peck on the cheek. "It looks as though we might be in for some nasty weather."

Indeed, a bitter wind was now whistling through the cracks of the McCallisters' old New England farmhouse. Through the parlor window, its 100-year-old glass panes rippled with age. Emmett watched as white falling snow was whipped into a frenzy.

Wouldn't you know, he thought, reaching for a log and thrusting it into the fire. **A Nor'easter, no less. And just in time for Christmas.**

"Christmas," he muttered scornfully, as though irritated by the word itself. "Hogwash."

With a "Harrumph!" worthy of Ebenezer Scrooge, Emmett reached up to straighten his collection of hand-carved and painted decoys that lined the rough-

hewn mantle above the fireplace. The fire-light flickering in the glass amber eyes of one mallard drake seemed to make the bird come alive. Gently Emmett stroked the duck's iridescent green head, letting his fingers trace the distinctive white ring that circled its neck like a clerical collar.

While Emmett may have hated Christmas, he loved birds.

His interest in ornithology first began when, as a boy of seven, he had nursed an injured baby robin back to health by feeding it with an eyedropper and keeping it warm in one of his father's fleece-lined slippers. Since then, Emmett had remained fascinated by birds—by their paradoxically delicate yet high-performance anatomy, by their wondrous ability to fly, by their mysterious instinct which enabled them to journey thousands of miles in uncanny synchronization with nature's changing rhythms. Now, his large yard was studded with assorted bird houses, baths, feeders, and suet bags.

"Honestly," Martha would often comment upon Emmett's return from one of his frequent trips to the local feed store—his arms aching under the weight of 25-

pound sacks of cracked corn and sunflower seeds—"sometimes I think you like those birds as much as people."

"Sometimes I do," he would reply.

Leaving the collection of decoys, Em-

39

mett returned to his easy chair. Piled high on the coffee table was the day's mail, for the most part a jumble of gaily-colored Christmas cards.

For unto you is born this day a Saviour, read one.

And the Word became flesh, and dwelt among us, read another.

"Hogwash," responded Emmett to the messages, pushing them aside to reach for his favorite bird magazine. The periodical had just arrived and he was eager to read it. But as he pulled the magazine onto his lap and saw its cover, his face fell.

It couldn't be said that the cover illustration was unusual in any way; that is, it was an exquisite rendering of two cardinals perched on a snow-covered pine bough. But the theme was obvious— **Christmas.** Emmett felt betrayed. Angry. Even his favorite magazine had sold out to the holiday season. Letting the magazine drop to the floor, he leaned back in his chair and closed his eyes.

What is it about Christmas that bothers me so? he wondered. **What is it about this time of year that makes other people so happy?**

Christmas, for Emmett, had been all right when his children had been small and living at home. He had no problem accepting Santa, and Rudolph, and stockings hung over the fireplace, and all the other trappings of the season. But when it came to the heart of the holiday—when it came to the issue of a baby called Jesus born nearly 2,000 years ago—that's when Emmett became very impatient. **What could such talk about God becoming human be, besides foolish religious prattle?** he thought. **And even if the story was true, why should such an event be necessary? Besides,** he concluded, **what had this Jesus ever done for me?**

The only time Emmett felt the least bit sorrowful for his inability to understand Christmas was when he was reminded—on nights like tonight—of how important this Jesus seemed to be to his wife Martha. Emmett loved his wife dearly and it bothered him when he perceived, albeit dimly, this great gulf that yawned between them. Sometimes he sensed that something was somehow missing in their relationship because he didn't share his wife's interest in religious matters. But

40

such feelings had always been too cloudy for him to talk about.

Suddenly, there was a commotion at the parlor window. A frantic fluttering of wings, piercing cries of distress—Emmett knew the sounds all too well. In a flash he was up, his face pressed against the cold glass, his eyes searching the dark night. Then, silhouetted by the glare of the front-porch floodlight, he saw what he was looking for—a small band of starlings, lost in the storm. Two of the six or seven birds had flown into the parlor window. Stunned by the impact, they now flopped about helplessly on the ground, their panicked movements digging them ever deeper into the fast-drifting snow.

Reaching for his windbreaker and pulling on his boots, Emmett stepped out on the front porch. The starlings grew even more distressed.

"No, no," murmured Emmett. "Please don't be scared. Don't be frightened. I'm here to help you. Please let me help you."

The starlings needed shelter, he realized. And fast. For the birds to remain unprotected in the bitter weather for much longer would surely result in their death.

Shielding his face against the blowing snow with his arm, Emmett pushed himself into the gale-force wind and trudged the 30-foot distance to his garage. He opened the door. If he could only get the starlings into the garage, he reasoned, then they would be safe.

But how to do it? he wondered, as he made his way back to the troubled birds. **The starlings were so frightened already; why should they trust me?**

For the next ten minutes, like an ungainly sheep dog, Emmett did his best to round up the starlings and herd them toward the garage. But his efforts were futile; there were too many birds. Like a shepherd needing a staff, Emmett needed some kind of instrument that would help him in his task.

He returned to the house to get a broom.

But, to Emmett's dismay, this approach met with results even more disastrous than the first. The starlings, already frightened and confused, responded in sheer terror to the broom by scattering in all different directions. Many fell into deep

snowbanks.

Heartsick and exhausted, Emmett finally realized the situation was hopeless. By morning, the starlings would all be dead.

Returning to the house, he draped his jacket, wet with snow, on the row of hooks by the front door and kicked off his boots. He returned to his easy chair and there, hanging his head, he wept. Bitterly he wept. As he hadn't wept since he was child, Emmett cried for his lost starlings.

Some time later, when he could cry no longer, Emmett heaved a shuddery sigh.

"God," he murmured, "if only I could become a bird. If only I could become a starling, so I could show those helpless creatures the way to safety and shelter. If only I could become one of them, then they would trust me. They would listen to me. Then—and only then—we could communicate with each other in a way never before possible."

Slowly, Emmett opened his eyes. Irresistibly, they were drawn to the pile of Christmas cards on the coffee table in front of him. For the second time that evening he considered their messages:

For unto you is born this day a Saviour . . .

And the Word became flesh, and dwelt among us . . .

Suddenly, Emmett's eyes filled with tears. No longer did the sight of Christmas cards annoy him. No longer did he despise this religious season. For now, at long last, with tears of joy, Emmett understood.

Just as Emmett loved and cared for his starlings so much that he wanted to become one of them in order to help them, so God loved humankind that He sent His only Son, Jesus, into the world to reveal Himself to all who would believe.

How simple, Emmett thought. **How wonderful!**

"Oh, thank You, God," he whispered, trembling with excitement at his new discovery. "Thank You for loving me so much that You sent Jesus to be born for me. Thank You for helping me understand the meaning of Christmas."

Abruptly, Emmett jumped at the sound of his name. It was his wife Martha, home from midnight mass.

"Emmett!" she cried. **"Emmett!"** Her

voice was high-pitched with excitement.

"What is it?" answered Emmett.

Suddenly Martha was in the parlor, her face flushed from running. Her boots left wet tracks on the hardwood floor, and she hadn't bothered to remove her coat or muffler.

"Emmett!" she exclaimed. "What are all those birds doing in our garage?"

"Birds?" asked Emmett with a puzzled look.

"Yes, birds," said Martha. "Six or seven of them. Starlings, I think. They're all perched up in the rafters, singing up a storm. And I'm afraid some of them must have gotten into your feed bags—there's seed spilled all over the floor. Honestly, Emmett," she shook her head, "I don't mind your birds as long as they stay outside, but when you start bringing them inside the house—"

"Starlings, you say?" Emmett's face was incredulous. "Six or seven?" It was too good to be true. Nothing short of God's own hand could have guided those half-frozen and confused birds into the garage.

"Yes," replied Martha. "That's what I said." She paused. "Emmett, you look strange. Emmett—are you all right?"

"All right?" cried Emmett, grabbing Martha around her plump waist and pulling her close. "All right? Martha, my dear, I've never been better! You may find this hard to believe, but there's been a miracle tonight. An honest-to-goodness miracle right here in own own house!"

"Miracle?" asked Martha. "But Emmett, you don't believe in miracles. You don't even believe in Christmas. What in heaven's name are you talking about?"

"There's been a miracle," repeated Emmett emphatically. "A Christmas miracle." Chuckling, he took Martha by the hand and led her down the hallway toward the garage. "Come on," he said. "Let's have a look at those starlings, and I'll tell you all about it."

MAY YOU HAVE JOY

May you have joy in the mad rush of
    preparation;
May you know peace in the tiny margins
    of time around the busy days;
May you have star-shine in clear night
    skies for looking at;
May you have silence now and then; and
    above all—beyond all else—
May you have love to give and to
    receive.

ELIZABETH SEARLE LAMB

44

THE BLESSING OF THE ANIMALS

Patricia Sullivan

My great-grandmother was born in a rural area of Ireland. She told me that during the great potato famine, no matter how poor her parents and their neighbors were, they always put out "a wee bit for the beasties" on Christmas Eve. This gift—this blessing—was given to the animals in honor of the role they played in the humble stable in Bethlehem.

So when we moved from the city to a farm in Wisconsin, my husband and I and our nine children decided to revive this family tradition.

At midnight, on Christmas Eve, we all troop down to the barn, through deep snow that crunches underfoot, and bring our gifts to the animals. We check to see that each animal has fresh water and clean bedding. Then the children take turns giving the horses and colts apples, carrots, oats and hay. The pigs are given extra mash and chopped vegetables. The cats and kittens, who have been playing around our feet, lap up big bowls of warm, frothy milk before getting little bags of catnip the girls have tied up in bundles for them. Our Irish setters Erin, Big Red and old Mike wait patiently for their treat of meat broth and scraps over dry dog food.

"You are a good and faithful friend," says our youngest daughter Patti to each animal in turn, petting it fondly. "We ask the blessing of the animals, in Jesus' Name."

When all the animals are fed and comfortable, we trudge back to our own snug home. The air is cold. The stars are bright. The night is silent. It is then that the holiness of Bethlehem's stable becomes very real to me. Our family sleeps then, I think, in heavenly peace.

THE LITTLE FIRES

Lorena Pepper Edlen

On Christmas Eve in El Paso, Texas, and throughout New Mexico, thousands, perhaps millions, of little fires are lighted to welcome the Christ Child into homes waiting to receive Him and to provide illumination so that no unseen obstacle will cause feet carrying Him to stumble.

The custom of lighting the fires started among Hispanic people many years ago and is observed chiefly in the Southwestern part of the United States. The little fires are called **luminarios.**

Perhaps one reason for their predominance in the Southwest is the abundance of available sand. Sand is one of the key ingredients in making **luminarios.** It provides support for the candles and prevents the little fires from becoming big fires if the wind comes up.

Making and setting out **luminarios** is usually a family project. They are made by folding down the top of a brown paper lunch sack to form a stiff cuff to hold the sack open, filling the sack about one-third full of sand, and inserting a cigar-size candle. The top of the flame comes below the top of the sack, like a lantern.

Luminarios are placed about two feet apart along a sidewalk, street curb, and walkways to a front door. Houses with brick or concrete steps have **luminarios** set on them. Houses with brick porch railings have **luminarios** strung across them. Some people even outline their tile roofs with **luminarios.**

At dusk on Christmas Eve, the entire family, plus any friends who can take on the chore, light the candles. Often whole neighborhoods get together and set out **luminarios** to welcome the Christ Child. They are much more effective when the little fires light up every walkway.

The candles turn the paper bags into patches of soft, yellow light. They burn until they reach the sand, perhaps three hours at most, and then go out, giving families attending Christmas Eve midnight mass ample time to get to church.

Lighting the way for the Christ Child requires a great deal of work, but it is a charming way of keeping Christ in Christmas.

THE MAGIC CHRISTMAS BELL

Wanda L. Jones

The weather was clear and cold as nine-year-old Melody left the school Christmas Bazaar with her single purchase—a tiny Christmas bell.

"It's a magic Christmas bell," the woman had said, a note of hushed wonder in her voice.

Melody did not believe in magic any more than she believed in Santa Claus or the tooth fairy.

"Every time it rings, they say, it brings a Christmas blessing, if the owner has the magic of Christmas."

"How do I know if I have this magic?" Melody had questioned. "Maybe the bell wouldn't work for me."

"It would be well worth finding out, wouldn't it? After all, what greater good is there than to give blessings to others?"

Even if it was just a plain Christmas bell with no magic at all, it was pretty and had a pure, sweet tone. It looked quite festive pinned now to her coat. As she jumped a snow drift, the bell gave a merry tinkle.

"Well, hello, little Christmas spirit. You sound like Christmas itself coming down the street." Mr. Swenson, the baker, was shoveling snow from the front of his shop.

"Reminds me of a little bell that used to hang on our Christmas tree when my daughter was a little girl. Whenever a draft would tremble the branches, the little bell would tinkle, and my daughter would call out from her bed, 'Is it Santa Claus, Papa?' " The old man's face clouded. "That was a very long time ago. My daughter and her family live far away now. I will not see them this Christmas.

But, here now. Won't you come inside the shop? I baked some Christmas cookies this morning."

Melody followed reluctantly, fearing that even a few minutes with this sad old man would only spoil the afternoon.

"They're almond cookies, my daughter's favorite," he went on as he put a plateful of the counter. "I don't know what I was thinking. Six dozen Christmas cookies on Christmas Eve, and the shop closed tomorrow! They will grow stale with only myself to eat them! Foolish old man." He wiped his eyes with the corner of his white apron.

In the warm, steamy bakery the two ate cookies, talked about Christmases past, and to Melody's surprise were soon laughing merrily. Mr. Swenson's eyes grew bright, and Melody knew he was no longer sad.

As she rose to go, Mr. Swenson put several more cookies into a bag. His wrinkled face broke into a smile.

"Such a blessing you have brought me today, little Christmas spirit! I was feeling sad and lonely, but I shouldn't have. I have so many happy things to think about and little friends like you to visit me. Perhaps I'll even decorate a Christmas tree tonight—with a little bell on it!" he added with a wink.

In spite of the cold, a warm feeling inside her persisted all the way down the block. Melody gave a little skip that set her Christmas bell to tinkling.

Suddenly she heard deep sobs. A little boy was sitting in the snow, his sled overturned. Melody bent over to help him up. The Christmas bell jingled merrily. The tear-streaked face looked up, and the red, swollen eyes fixed themselves on the bell.

Melody jingled the bell again with her finger. "Do you like my bell?" she asked, smiling. "It's a magic bell, you know."

The little boy's eyes grew round with wonder.

"Is it really magic?" he asked shyly.

"For sure," Melody said emphatically, taking his hand. "Come on. I'll walk you home. You mustn't cry on Christmas Eve. It's a happy day."

Four houses down, she left the little boy at his door.

"What kind of magic does it do?" he asked, still awed by the bell.

"It makes things disappear," she replied.

"Like what, for instance?"

"Well, your tears, for one thing. They're all gone."

The boy laughed, squeezed her hand, and disappeared inside.

"Well, little bell, if you don't work wonders! Even if it isn't real magic," Melody said aloud as she headed homeward again.

On the corner a man was standing motionless. Melody knew by the red-tipped cane he held that he was blind. As she made a turn to go around him, her little Christmas bell tinkled sweetly.

"Who's there?" he called out, tilting his head to one side.

"Only me," Melody answered timidly. She did not make a habit of talking to strangers.

"Come here, please," he pleaded. "I've been standing here for quite a long time waiting for someone to help me. You see, I've dropped something in the snow, and I fear I may have covered it up looking for it. Would you take a look? It is a brooch, a very special brooch, for my wife. I must find it."

Melody knelt and began to brush away the snow. She soon found the brooch and placed it in the grateful man's hands.

"How can I thank you? You have saved me from a very unhappy Christmas. It was a blessing you came along when you did."

Another Christmas blessing! thought Melody. She waited for the walk light and bounded across the intersection toward St. Luke's Church. Father Jackson stood on the steps.

"Father Jackson, could I ask you something?" Melody began.

"Of course, Melody," the priest answered, "What is it?"

"Just one question, Father. Is there . . . could there be magic in a Christmas bell?"

"Magic in a bell?" The priest looked puzzled.

Briefly she told him the woman's claim about the bell. "And it's happened three times on the way home," she said, detailing her encounters. "Three times it rang and three times someone got a blessing. The woman said it would happen if I had the magic of Christmas. Do I have it, Father Jackson?''

The priest's face softened. "You do, indeed, Melody. You gave three blessings, sure as the world.''

"Then it's true? The bell is magic?''

"No, not the bell, little one. The 'magic,' as the woman told you truthfully, is in you. It's love. That's the magic of Christmas. When you give love to those you meet, you give blessings indeed.''

Melody turned toward home, her steps picking up speed. She wanted to think about what Father Jackson had said, but not now. She was too excited, and she felt unusually happy.

She did not notice that the priest was still looking after her or that the tension of a too-busy Christmas was gone from his face. Neither did she hear his words that were swept away by the wind.

"Keep working that magic, little one, and you will discover the real blessing it brings—the happiness that comes to the heart of the one who gives love.''

GOD'S CHRISTMAS
AUTOGRAPH

On Christmas Eve I saw
   God's autograph in the snow—
Tiny creature tracks so fine,
   All lacy in a row.

And with the dazzling Christmas
   dawn,
   My eyes did then behold.
God's signature grown ever dear,
   Etched in sunlight gold.

ROSALYN HART FINCH

THE FLOWER OF CHRISTMAS EVE

Shirley Climo

Not too long ago, in a certain Mexican village, it was the custom to bring offerings to the Christ Child on Christmas Eve. The villagers crowded the candlelit church and placed their presents by the manger scene, or **nacimiento.** Each brought what he could: a measure of the harvest, a freshly baked **pan dulce** (sweet bun), a few coins, a garland of flowers.

One boy, small and poor, had nothing to give. So he picked some weeds that grew in the dust of the churchyard. The other worshippers scorned his straggly weeds, and would have swept them away.

But as the child laid his branches beside the manger, the church was filled with a light far brighter than that of the flickering candles. For each green stalk suddenly blazed red, centered with golden flowers that glowed like the Christmas Star. The miracle of love made the boy's gift the most wonderful of all.

This plant still spreads its crimson bracts at Christmastime. We call it the **poinsettia.** And to our Latin neighbors it is the "Flor de la Noche Buena"—the "Flower of the Holy Night."

O HOLY NIGHT

O holy night! The stars are brightly
  shining,
It is the night of the dear Savior's birth;
Long lay the world in sin and error
  pining,
Till He appeared and the soul felt its
  worth.
A thrill of hope the weary world rejoices,
For yonder breaks a new and glorious
  morn.

Fall on your knees
Oh, hear the angel voices!
O night divine
O night when Christ was born!
O night
O holy night, O night divine!

JUST LIKE OTHER FAMILIES

Van Varner

Christmas Eve at our house. Snowflakes falling on the lawn as softly as fine feathers; a circle of prickly green on the front door; a fat Norwegian pine twinkling with lights in the living room; and in the dining room, a silent night. Very silent. Nobody at the table talking to anybody.

Why, I asked myself as I took another taste of my mother's special-occasion mushroom soup, **why can't my family be like other families?**

I was the sentimental one. I yearned for these holiday times when the six of us were fully assembled, but I wanted peace to reign. Fat chance in our house. Certainly not this Christmas anyway. Already everything had gone wrong.

I slipped a glance about the dining-room table. The table was round, a fact which was of special meaning to Mom. "A round table," she was fond of saying, "brings us all closer together." Yet tonight we were a tableful of distant relatives. Hal, my older brother, sat next to me, wielding his spoon as though he and the soup were in competition. Hal was the athletic one. And he was scowling. It had just been revealed, finally and definitely, that when we descended the stairs on Christmas morning a number of presents would be awaiting him, but the rifle he wanted would not be one of them. Dad, who was the firm one, had pressed Hal's case with Mom about this, but Mom, who was the firmer one, was not about to allow a gun in the house. So Hal sulked.

So did Dad.

Dad was not in a good mood anyway. He'd already had his first tiff of the holiday with my grandmother. And he'd had trouble getting home from the office. The Studebaker had slithered on the ice coming up Hogback Hill and two sets of chains had broken on him. "I think my hands are frozen," he'd yelled at Mom when he came in the door. He said it as though not having any gloves was her fault. His hands were not frozen.

The quietest person at the table was my grandmother. She was the grand one. She was very beautiful, or so everyone was always saying, and because she was very beautiful she required a considerable amount of attention. Dad called her The Queen. Her comings and goings were always regal events, to which her mid-afternoon arrival could attest. The door bell had rung, the door was opened, and there she stood, a queen in Persian lamb with an additional cluster of fur, a fascinating fox with head and paws still attached, about her neck. For a long time she did not cross the threshold, choosing rather to stand **in** it, keeping the taxi driver who had struggled up with her luggage out,

letting the cold air in.

"My dear ones!" she'd cried, flinging open her arms with a generous invitation for us to come to them. And when we did, Mom and my brothers and I, she swaddled us in hugs and kisses and left no possible doubt as to her great joy in seeing us again. But after the kisses and the joy came the report of her trip, which had been "Ghastly, utterly ghastly!" with invisible redcaps, no heat in the Pullman, the train behind schedule, and she was about to write to the president of the railroad.

In no time, though, things had settled down to normal, and Gran was coming down the stairs asking Mom to send someone immediately to fix whatever was wrong with the window shade in her bedroom, and then down the stairs again to

insist upon a little quiet so she could nap. At that point she'd run into Dad, who was having his frozen-hands problem, and though he kissed her on the cheek and said he was glad to see her, he said that quiet was something she could not expect in our house and she'd better learn to nap in the din. He also said that when in Rome she should "do as the Romans do."

"I've been to Rome," was Gran's reply, "and I **did not** do as they did then, **nor** will I now." That led to other words, which came out louder and louder, until Gran removed herself to her bedroom and refused to come out. Eventually my younger brother Jo-Jo was dispatched to woo her down for dinner. Jo-Jo was the charming one. And in the end Gran did indeed respond to his charms, but she sat at the table now in refrigerated silence.

"I hope the snow won't keep us from midnight service," Mom said, trying to say something, anything, to start a conversation.

"I don't want to go to church," Hal said.

"You are going to go whether you want to or not," Dad told him.

"But only if the roads are safe, dear," Mom added. I looked at her as she spoke. She was the tired one. Now she stood up and motioned me to help her clear the soup plates. After two trips to the pantry, I came back to my chair and sat. Hal drummed his fingers on the table. Gran stared hard at nothing.

"Thump!" came a heavy crashing sound from the kitchen, then a clatter. We looked at one another, but no one moved. We waited for a report from Mom. There was none. A minute, two minutes went by. Dad was the first to slip away from the table, then Hal and I got up simultaneously and pushed open the door to the kitchen.

Mom was sitting at the breakfast table with her head in her hands. She was crying. I was astonished. Mom never cried. On the kitchen floor by the oven lay an overturned broiling pan. In an ever-widening pool of hot grease sprawled a huge, embarrassed-looking turkey.

"It just slipped out of my hands," Mom said between sobs. "I wanted everything to be so nice, but everything, **everything** has gone wrong."

Dad looked nervous. He tried to reassure her, pointing out how hard she'd been working, how Christmasy the house looked. "Who cares what the house looks like?" Mom said suddenly, sharply, sitting up straight. Now the whole family was in the kitchen, standing like awkward spectators at a car accident. "Does anyone here really **want** Christmas? Does anyone of you really **care?** No, the only thing we care about is ourselves, and that is everything Christmas should **not** be."

No one said a word. We just stood there.

"I care," said my grandmother in a strong voice that I'd never heard before. "I care enough to come hundreds of miles to have Christmas with my family, and Christmas is what we are going to have. Now wipe those tears and go back to the dining room. All of you. Scat!"

I think I'd never seen my grandmother in an apron before, but now she put one on and took charge of the kitchen in a way I'd never thought possible. In an extraor-

dinary reversal of roles, Mom became the waited-upon, and in no time Dad was carving the rescued turkey and we were passing creamed onions and parsnips and cranberry sauce. Hal smiled at Dad, shyly. Jo-Jo kicked me under the table. I was about to punch him back when he grinned, "Merry Christmas, Brother." Then he made one of his famous Jo-Jo statements:

"This is like the first Christmas, isn't it?"

We weren't quite sure what he meant.

"I mean," he explained, "things went wrong for Mary and Joseph too, didn't they?"

There was a long silence. I thought about the long trip from Galilee to Bethlehem, Mary heavy with child, the confusion of finding a place to stay, the rejection at door after door, the cold of the night, the darkness of the stable . . .

"Everything went wrong for them too," Jo-Jo declared, "but everything turned out just fine—like it has for us."

We all laughed. Dad reached over and touched Gran's hand. Mom beamed at all of us.

Later, at the candle-lit service in church, for the first time as long as I could remember, we all sat together in the same pew: Mom and Dad, Gran, Jo-Jo, Hal and I.

As I said, I'm the sentimental one. Later, at the candle-lit service in church, when I saw the nativity scene near the altar, I felt a new sense of kinship with the little Christmas family. And when I looked down the row and saw Mom and Dad and Gran and Hal and Jo-Jo—all of us sitting together in the same pew for the first time in as long as I could remember—I wanted to shout out my happiness. Here we were, six of us living through the strains and stresses that give life its substance, six individuals held together in spite of ourselves by the mysterious force of love, just like other families.

THE LIGHT FROM THE CAVE

Sidney Fields

The innkeeper's wife, small and timid, was telling the story to her incredulous neighbors:

"You never saw such a light. And it wrought such strange events. How can I ever describe it?

"Do you remember that night last week when the town was so crowded? Everyone wanted a room. But we had none left. Zara, whose brother had struck my husband, was pleading with my husband not to press charges.

"Into this confusion came the man Joseph and his wife, Mary. She was but a girl. When Joseph asked for a room, my husband vented his anger upon him. Joseph bowed his head, and pointed to the cave outside.

" 'Might we use the cave?' he begged. 'My wife is to be delivered of a child soon. We will not disturb the animals.'

" 'Go elsewhere,' my husband said.

"In shame I followed Joseph outside to comfort him. His wife smiled gently, though she was troubled. It was no ordinary face. Quickly, without knowing why, I told them to use the cave. Suddenly, there was a new strength in me. I feared not my husband's anger, though I could hear him shouting at Zara, 'Your brother tried to rob me. He will be stoned to death!' And Zara was pleading, 'Have you no forgiveness?'

"It was the servant boy on an errand for my husband who later discovered Joseph and Mary in the cave. My husband, his face white with anger, followed by Zara, quickly came out toward the cave. But their steps faltered. It was the soft cry of the Child that halted them.

"Mary held the Babe while Joseph knelt beside her. The radiance of Mary's face was bright. But still brighter was the light from the dark cave.

"A Child was born. And love was born then, too. For my husband's eyes filled with torment, and he spoke softly. 'Zara,' he said, 'ask your brother to forgive me.'

"And the light shone even brighter. Will you come and see it? The light is still there although the man, his wife and the Child are gone. I think the light will shine forever."

A CHRISTMAS GIFT TO EVERYONE

Our Father up in heaven, long,
   long years ago.
Looked down in His great mercy
   upon the earth below
And saw that folks were lonely
   and lost in deep despair
And so He said, "I'll send My
   Son to walk among them
   there . . .
So they can hear Him speaking
   and feel His nearness, too,
And see the many miracles that
   faith alone can do—
For if man really sees Him and
   can touch His healing hand
I know it will be easier to believe
   and understand."

HELEN STEINER RICE

A BONNIE BRAE CHRISTMAS

Bill Deerfield

The first faint light of dawn was silhouetting the dark hills beyond Bonnie Brae Farm. I was only 13 years old and it was my fourth month at Bonnie Brae, a home for boys from broken families near Morristown, New Jersey.

Life for a "new boy" like me was very hard. It was bad enough being shy and all, but the other boys seemed unfriendly and mean. They'd laugh at me, tease me and once they even hid my clothes. At night there would be gravel in my bed or I'd find it had been short-sheeted.

My chief tormentor was Joe. He was the biggest and toughest boy in the cottage. He was older, too, and I both feared and admired him.

"Hey, look . . ." he sneered to the other boys around the breakfast table one morning, proudly displaying **my** corn muffin perched atop his fork for all to see. The boys laughed and cheered. "Hey guys—I think the baby's going to cry!" he said mockingly, flicking the muffin back on my plate. I stared at the broken muffin crumbled all over my eggs and bacon. My eyes watered, but I fought back the tears, gripping my fork with Samson-like intensity.

And so it went . . . day after day. Joe never seemed to let up. No matter how much I tried to be nice afterwards—I didn't want to be a poor sport and hoped he'd just ignore me—inside I was smouldering with resentment.

Now it was Christmas Day. Deep inside I knew this was going to be the most miserable Christmas I could ever have. I dragged myself out of bed and surprisingly made it through breakfast without incidence. Joe and the other boys were so busy chattering away about the presents they hoped to get that afternoon from Santa that they forgot about me. I was relieved and for once finished breakfast without a mess or being messed up!

At two o'clock that afternoon, the doors to the large dining hall were opened and I filed in with the rest of the boys for Christmas dinner. I tried to be cheerful, but I had my guard up. No telling what Joe and the boys might be up to now.

The big room was warm and festive, hung with pine wreaths and garlands. Even the moosehead over the fireplace—usually the target of butter patties catapulted from the cutlery—was decked out with holly and red ribbons. Under the big tree, ablaze with lights, was a huge pile of presents. My boy's heart was so taken with the Christmas festivities that I forgot about Joe and settled into enjoying din-

ner. We had turkey with all the fixins', mince pie for dessert and glasses and glasses of creamy milk straight from our own dairy—Christmas was turning out to be not so bad!

Then Santa arrived and began handing out presents. I wondered if I would get what I asked for. My name was called and I blushed deeply. I walked across the newly-polished floor toward Santa. His bright eyes twinkled as he handed me a small, oblong box wrapped in red, shiny paper tied with a gold bow. Excitedly, I resumed my place back at the table and began unwrapping the package.

There—right before my eyes—it was! **The watch! The watch I had asked for!** Inside I bubbled with delight. Never before had I been so happy. My fingers picked it up. Its solid weight sank into the palm of my hand. My eyes traced the fine black numbers which gave it dignity; the second hand which circled its face with precision; and the rich brown leather which made the band thick and sturdy. I loved it. It was the most beautiful watch I had ever seen.

I held it up to my ear. **It wasn't ticking!** I looked closely through its clear, glass face—the second hand stopped moving. My heart sank.

"Here, let me see it," Joe said, slipping up behind me and grabbing the watch. I froze in silence as the treasured gift disappeared from my grip. I held my breath as Joe danced off with it. A group quickly huddled around him and my coveted watch was hidden in what seemed to be a forest of gangling, gawking boys.

Silently, I sat by myself at the empty table afraid to move. My eyes stared at the cluster of boys, but there was no sign of my trusty watch—only giggles and whispers coming from the "inner circle," heads bobbing up and down, and penetrating eyes glaring at me from time to time. Beads of sweat slid down my temples; it seemed as if hours had gone by.

Finally, I turned back around in my seat and looked at the empty watch case on the table. **I've lost it,** I said resignedly. **I've lost it for good.** I slumped my head in my hands, and this time I didn't care what Joe would think—the tears came and I

didn't even try to hide them.

I reached for the napkin in front of me and dabbed my eyes dry. I felt a tap on my shoulder. "Hey, Deerfield," Joe said, standing over me, "don't you know you gotta wind this thing?" He held it down in front of me showing me how. "But not too tight, you see, or it'll break!" He handed it back to me.

I was stunned. "You mean—"I said trembling, "you mean, you're not going to keep it?"

"Hey, it's **Christmas,** Deerfield," Joe said straightening up and standing tall. "What do you think Christmas is all about—if it ain't being nice? Besides, what kind of a guy do you think I am, anyway?" He looked real serious.

"But, Joe," I said puzzled, "I thought . . ."

"You thought what?" Joe interrupted me. "Listen, Deerfield, you're not a new guy anymore. You been here too long, so you better get used to it. No more special treatment from me or the boys, get it?" I shook my head in disbelief. Joe walked away.

"Hey, Bill," Joe called from across the room, "It's a nice watch—you better take good care of it!"

"You bet, Joe," I called back sporting my widest grin. **I ain't a new guy anymore,** I whispered. **Imagine that!**

That night our house mother, Mom Strang, took us boys out for Christmas Eve caroling on the porch. We craned our necks as she pointed out lots of different stars to us. They spangled in the black December sky like nature's own Christmas lights.

"Star of wonder, star of light . . . Star with royal beauty bright . . ." Mom sang in her high, nasal voice, sounding like a mountain woman. Nobody snickered. We all joined in.

"You better sing loud, Deerfield," Joe said, and his punch on my arm was light and friendly. I sang loudly and lustily, because at all once I was supremely happy.

Had it only been that morning that I had felt so miserable about being here? Now, I was filled with wondrous awe at my first Christmas at Bonnie Brae. Yes, this was my new home, but I wasn't a "new boy" anymore—**I belonged.** I was part of a great big family, with 85 brothers—my Bonnie Brae family.

"Joe," I whispered, leaning over towards him, "you think in the morning you could show me again how to wind my new watch?" Joe winked at me.

". . . Westward leading, still proceeding . . . Guide us to thy Perfect Light?" We sang into the frosty night air, while the stars twinkled overhead.

THE LAST BUS

Doris Crandall

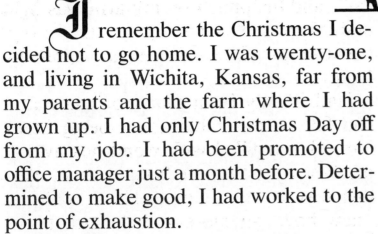

I remember the Christmas I decided not to go home. I was twenty-one, and living in Wichita, Kansas, far from my parents and the farm where I had grown up. I had only Christmas Day off from my job. I had been promoted to office manager just a month before. Determined to make good, I had worked to the point of exhaustion.

I'd welcome a day to myself. I'd attend a Christmas morning service, relax in the afternoon. If I went home I'd have to ride a Greyhound bus all night. I'd arrive in Shamrock, Texas, a small town nearest to the farm, at 6:00 a.m., and then in order to return to work the day after Christmas, I'd have to reverse the ride that night.

Not one to do things on the spur of the moment, I had sent Mama's and Daddy's gifts well ahead of time along with a letter saying how much I loved them and how much I missed them.

At that time, I could contact my parents only by mail. There was no telephone service to the farm, and Western Union didn't deliver messages to rural areas.

Having made the decision not to go home, I dug into my work and tried to forget that I wouldn't even be able to call my parents on Christmas Day.

At 5:30 on Christmas Eve, I wished my boss and co-workers a Merry Christmas and left the annual office party early.

On the way home I had to pass the Greyhound bus terminal. As I neared it, my steps slowed. When I saw the bus with "Oklahoma City" across the front, homesickness clutched my heart. I leaned against the building. **That's the last bus out to get me home by tomorrow morning,** I thought.

Woefully, I watched the passengers board the bus. The driver, taking tickets at the door, was one that I had ridden with several times before. When the last person got on, he looked my way.

"Hey, Sunshine, are you going or not?" he teased as he motioned and smiled.

My heart leaped. "I'm going," I said quickly. "Wait until I get a ticket."

Breathless, and tingling with happiness at the prospect of home, I settled into the only available seat. A short time later I wondered whatever had possessed me to make that snap decision. I hadn't even a change of clothing. And worse, since Mama and Daddy didn't know I was coming, how would I get the fifteen miles from Shamrock to the farm? I'd have to hitchhike, but who would be driving down the country road at six o'clock on Christmas morning?

In the dim, early morning light, the bus pulled into the Shamrock station. About now, I thought, Mama and Daddy are in the kitchen. Mama has lit the gas cook stove and left the oven door open to help warm the room. They are having a cup of coffee before Daddy goes to the barn to milk the cows. While he's gone Mama will cook sausage, eggs, and hot biscuits with butter and syrup. It's Daddy's favorite breakfast.

As I stepped off the bus, a woman threw her arms around me and I was in Mama's arms. "How did you know to meet the bus?" I asked as I wiped the tears from my eyes. "I wrote you I wasn't coming home."

"The truth is," Mama admitted, "we both had strong feelings that you'd be on this bus. After all, it **is** the last bus before Christmas."

Then I told them about my irresistible and last minute urge to hop onto that bus. Had we unknowingly sent each other mental dispatches?

"No," Mama said thoughtfully, "I don't think so. I believe God just put it on our hearts. It's one of His Christmas miracles. Let's go home."

Of all my memories of Christmases spent with Mama and Daddy, the year that I was impelled to take the-last-bus-before-Christmas home is my favorite one.

PART III
Christmas Stories
and Poems

"Behold . . ."

". . . behold Wise Men from the East came to Jerusalem saying, 'Where is He who is born King of the Jews? For we have seen His star in the East and have come to worship Him.' . . . And lo, the star which they had seen in the East went before them, till it came to rest over the place where the Child was. When they saw the star, they rejoiced with great joy; and going into the house they fell down and worshiped Him . . ."

MATTHEW 2:1-2, 9-11

A CHRISTMAS PRAYER FOR CHILDREN

Peter Marshall

Lord Jesus, who didst take little children into Thine arms and laugh and play with them, bless, we pray Thee, all children at this Christmastide. As with shining eyes and glad hearts they nod their heads so wisely at the stories of the angels, and of a baby cradled in the hay at the end of the way of a wandering star, may their faith and expectation be a rebuke to our own faithlessness.

Help us to make this season all joy for them, a time that shall make Thee, Lord Jesus, even more real to them. Watch tenderly over them and keep them safe. Grant that they may grow in health and strength into Christian maturity. May they turn early to Thee, the Friend of children, the Friend of all. We ask in the lovely name of Him who was once a little child. Amen.

HARK! THE HERALD ANGELS SING

Hark! the herald angels sing
Glory to the new-born King;
Peace on earth and mercy mild,
God and sinners reconciled!
Joyful all ye nations rise,
Join the triumph of the skies;
With th' angelic host proclaim,
Christ is born in Bethlehem.

Christ, by highest heav'n adored,
Christ, the everlasting Lord;
Late in time behold Him come,
Offspring of the Virgin's womb.
Veiled in flesh the God head see;
Hail th' Incarnate Deity,
Pleased as man with man to dwell,
Jesus our Emmanuel!

Hark! the herald angels sing
Glory to the new-born King!

THE LITTLEST SHEPHERD

Glenn Kittler

The small boy struggled to keep pace with the man. He said, "Please, Father, not so fast. I am getting tired."

But the man said, "Hurry, boy. I want to find out what all the excitement is about. Don't you hear the music?"

The boy strained to listen. "Music? I don't hear any music. Where is it coming from?"

"Everywhere," said the man. "It seems to be coming from the skies. I've never heard such singing. Hurry, son."

Panting, struggling, the boy said, "But Father, what about our flock? We have left the sheep alone. Shall I go back and guard them?"

The man shook his head. "No. The sheep will be all right. Look. **All** the shepherds have left their flocks."

The boy looked about. Sure enough, many other shepherds were hurrying up the steep hill, their faces beaming with joy and excitement. The boy asked, "Do they hear the singing, too?"

"Of course. Can't you? It is beautiful."

"No."

"Listen. 'Glory to God in the highest; and on earth, peace, goodwill toward men.' It is beautiful."

The boy shook his head. Why couldn't he hear the music?

The boy and the man reached the top of the hill and, with the others, went quickly to the edge of the town. They came to a small inn, where others had gathered, and they went around to the back of it, to the stable that was there. Many people were at the door, trying to see in.

The man asked another shepherd, "What is it? What is it?"

The shepherd answered, "Do you hear the music?"

"Of course. But what is it?"

The shepherd said, "A child was born in this stable tonight. Some say he is the Savior, the Messiah."

"The Messiah born in a stable?"

"Yes. As it was written many years ago."

"I must see this for myself." The man turned to the boy. "Son, you wait here.

I'm going to try to get inside."

The boy stepped away, into the darkness. He stood there a long time, watching the many excited people come and go, wondering what the shepherd had meant; wondering, too, why everyone seemed to be able to hear the music—everyone but him.

The cold night sent a chill through him. The boy was wearing a jacket made from the wool of his father's sheep. Now he tugged at the laces to bring the coat tighter around himself, warming him.

Finally he saw his father come out of the stable, looking about for him. The man called, "Son, come. We must hurry home and tell the rest of the family about this."

"About what?" called the boy. But his father had already turned and was hurrying down the road. The boy wondered, "About what?" And he knew he would have to see for himself.

The boy waited in the darkness until all the other people had gone and there was a quiet over the place. Then he went, slowly and unsure, to the stable door. It was dark, save for a slight glow at the far end. Timidly, the boy walked forward toward the light.

And he saw them. A young woman—still a girl, actually—looking down at a baby, swaddled in some cloths, lying in straw in a makeshift cradle. Nearby was an older man, watching the woman and the child intently.

The young woman noticed the shepherd boy. "Yes, my child?"

The boy said, "Can I see the baby?"

"Of course. Come closer."

The boy moved closer to the crib. To be sure, a glow seemed to be encircling the child. The boy said, "He looks very nice."

"Thank you."

"What's his name?"

The woman said, "He will be known as Jesus."

The boy nodded, still looking at the infant. "I heard someone say Messiah. I don't know what that means."

"You will understand when you are older, I'm sure."

"May I touch him?"

"Yes. Feel his hand. See how small it is."

The shepherd boy put a finger to the baby's hand and the baby gripped it. The boy grinned. "He's strong." Then the boy noticed that the baby wore only swad-dling cloths, and asked, "Is the baby warm enough?"

The young woman said, "It is all we have now."

The boy said, "I will give him my wooden coat. It will keep him warm."

"But you will need the coat yourself," the woman said.

"The baby needs it now more than I do," the boy said, and he took off his coat and tucked it about the baby. "Let it be his first birthday present," he whispered.

The woman smiled. "If you wish. And I am sure that when he is older he will give you a gift, too.

Suddenly the shepherd boy's face lit up, astonishment upon his face. "I hear music! I hear it! It sounds like singing! Can the baby hear the singing?"

"Yes," said the young woman. "I'm sure he hears it. And that he hears you—and always will."

A COLD NEW YORK CHRISTMAS

Dina Donohue

When he ran away from home, Jon Tyler vowed he'd never think of Vermont or the stepfather who made his life so unhappy.

"He's too strict," Jon complained to his mother.

As always, she sided with her husband. "Bill is only doing what's best for you."

When Bill took Jon's driving privilege away for staying out too late one night and letting his school grades slip, Jon emptied his savings account and headed for New York City and independence. He sent a postcard home as soon as he found a job, telling his mother not to worry.

He had been in the city for two months now but he was still a stranger. People were cold and distant. The only ones he talked to were the other busboys at the fast food restaurant where he worked. He had a room at the "Y" but hadn't made any friends there.

It was his day off and one of the busboys had said, "You ought to see the tree in Rockefeller Center." He stood beneath the giant tree, sparkling with its tiny colored lights. He was surrounded by throngs of happy people, he watched the skaters on the rink below, he took in the decorations in the surrounding stores—and felt more lonely and miserable than ever. No one gave him a glance or a smile.

He shivered from the cold and headed for the warmth of a Fifth Avenue department store. It was a large store, but impersonal and distant despite the holiday decorations and Christmas music coming from overhead speakers.

People pushed past him, irritable clerks rang up sales. In Vermont, a customer would be greeted warmly by the owner of the store or the salesperson.

He walked through the aisles, amazed at the array of jewelry, scarves, purses and other gift items on display.

But he couldn't shake his desire to go home. It wasn't only the lack of fare money which gnawed at him. Maybe his mother and Bill wouldn't care if he didn't come back. Maybe they were happier without him.

It was just at this moment, with sudden tears clouding his eyes, that he bumped inito a table piled high with leather wallets. Table, wallets and Jon crashed to the floor.

Stunned but not hurt, Jon lay outstretched on the floor until a security guard pulled him to his feet. He was half-carried to an office where a grim faced man sat behind a massive desk.

Questions came one after the other: had he been alone? . . . why did he knock over the table? . . . would he voluntarily empty his pockets or should they call the police? . . . where were his friends?

"I just didn't look where I was going. I'm sorry," Jon protested. "I don't have any friends. I'm no thief." He willingly emptied his pockets.

The man behind the desk glared at him. "During the Christmas rush we have all sorts of people pulling tricks to steal merchandise. Crashing a table is one way to get attention away from a confederate staging a robbery nearby."

"No, I just came in to get warm. I was cold." And then, although he couldn't understand why he confided in this stern man, Jon said: "I bumped into the table because I was dreaming about going home to Vermont for Christmas. I ran away two months ago and I don't know if they want me back. Anyway, I have no money for fare."

The man's face softened. He reached for the telephone on his desk. "What's your home phone number, son?"

And a stranger in a cold, impersonal New York City store sent Jon Tyler home for Christmas where he was indeed wanted.

Since the first Christmas when a Son was the most welcomed of all babies, homecoming at Christmas has been a blessed and cherished tradition.

OH LORD . . .

Oh Lord, this is a season of light,
   of Bethlehem candles burning.
Help me to bask in that light
   and in that full radiance
   see my brother as he really is.

Help me to sustain that
   recognition of him
As the seasons turn
   and the night sky, once more,
Is aburst with the
   brilliance of Your birth.

         Amen

            GORDON NEEL

GOD'S CANDLES

God, light tall candles in my heart.
   Make every dim-lit space
So glowing that no evil thing
   Can find a hiding place.

God, light tall candles in my heart.
   Lest I should fail to see
That Thy Word is the cup of strength
   For all humanity.

Burn brightly, candles in my heart. . . .
   No soul has ever trod
Earth's twisted way in faith without
   Deeper inner light from God.

            GERTUDE HANSON

THE CHRISTMAS THAT CHANGED A TOWN'S NAME

Martin Buxbaum

River Fork was a small town, a friendly town, except for the Fletchers and the McCloskeys. They hadn't spoken to each other for two generations. No one seemed to know why they hated each other, not even the Fletchers and the Mc-Closkeys. But the Fletchers did not speak to the McCloskeys and the McCloskeys did not speak to the Fletchers.

One night shortly before one Christmas something happened to change that and anyone who was there will tell you what made the citizens of River Fork also change their town's name.

It all began one November morning when plump, motherly, Mrs. Parris happily made an announcement to her fifth grade class: "This coming Christmas, children, our class has been selected to give a Christmas Play! We will begin choosing those who will play various parts and everyone will have **some** part in the play." Upon hearing this, the children clapped and squealed.

And so the players were selected and each child who had a speaking part was given a simple script.

The sixth graders were given the job of making the stage scenery. The seventh graders would play the music and parents would, as usual, be asked to make the costumes and provide refreshments. Mrs. Parris was determined to make this the best Christmas play the school had ever

put on.

The list went on . . . Mr. Loveliss had agreed to lend a small, gentle burro and Mr. Baker promised to provide straw for the stable from his grain and feed store. One thing bothered Mrs. Parris, however—the infant Jesus. In almost all Nativity plays, a doll was used in the manger. But Mrs. Parris wanted it to be really special . . . the infant should be a real child. But who would lend a new baby for the school play? She decided to ask her students what **they** thought. She'd learned long ago that children were smarter than grown-ups believed they were—especially if given the opportunity to express themselves.

She asked her class what **they** thought of her idea of a live baby for the play, and the children all agreed—they wanted a real baby to be in the manger. That settled it. So next she asked if anyone had a baby brother. Only one hand was raised. It was Amanda Fletcher. "Yes, Amanda? Do **you** have a small baby brother?"

"No, ma'am, but I have a baby sister. She's three months old and she never cries."

Aaron McCloskey snorted. "Jesus wasn't a girl. That's dumb. A girl for the Baby Jesus!"

"Now wait a moment, children," said Mrs. Parris. "The baby will be in a manger, so no one will **know** if it's a boy or girl. I shall call your mother tonight, Amanda."

That night Mrs. Parris phoned Mrs. Fletcher who listened, then said: "Amanda already told me of the Christmas play. She's delighted she was chosen to play the part of Mary and more delighted that you want Christina to be the Infant Jesus."

"**Christina**—oh, how beautiful! And so appropriate," said Mrs. Parris.

Mrs. Fletcher sighed. "There is something we haven't told Amanda yet. We took Christina to the doctor last week . . ." Her voice broke slightly. "The doc-

79

tor says Christina has no voice. She cannot cry, nor will she ever be able to speak."

Mrs. Parris was stunned. "I'm **so** sorry."

"I thought you should know. But if you still want Christina in the play, I shall bring her. With Amanda so near, I'm sure the baby won't be upset."

On the night of the play, little Christina lay in the manger, squirming and kicking her feet for all to see. She actually seemed to enjoy the attention.

At the climax of the play, the stage lights dimmed except for one spotlight focused on the manger. The figures of Joseph, Mary and the Wise Men knelt in prayer. Offstage, the chorus began to sing, "It Came Upon the Midnight Clear . . ." And as they sang, the baby's arms waved.

As the last notes of the old song died away, Aaron McCloskey, dressed as an angel wearing dark horn-rimmed glasses, came out on stage. A blue spotlight held him in its light. He spread his arms wide and in a loud, high-pitched voice recited flatly, "May the Holy Birth bring joy into the hearts of each and every one of us this

Christmas!"

He was supposed to leave the stage at this point, but instead, all the thoughts that had long been buried inside the boy came rushing out. In a voice that was now filled with genuine emotion he added: "And may my parents and Amanda's parents be friends again!" He turned and ran from the stage.

There was a stunned silence in the auditorium. From the rear of the auditorium someone said "Amen," and the applause began. Then, as if in agreement, a small cry came from the manger and a tiny arm waved vigorously.

Mrs. Fletcher leaped to her feet and raced onto the stage. She picked up the wailing Christina and held her up for all to see. "Praise God," she shouted, "it's a miracle!"

Word spread quickly about the miracle, for no one had known about Christina's condition. The following Sunday, everyone in River Fork was in church. The Fletchers and McCloskeys shared the same pew and Amanda hoped Christina wouldn't disturb the service.

Reverend Adams stepped to the pulpit. "Friends, I'm not going to try to understand or explain what happened in the school auditorium last night. But we sure saw a couple of miracles happen." He stared directly at the McCloskeys and Fletchers.

"I want to propose that we do something to remind us all of this great wonder. I propose we change the name of our town from River Fork to—Miracle."

The shouts and applause were enough to convince everyone it was a good idea.

Once again a baby had reached into the hearts of people and left the priceless gift of love. And to this day it's said you'll never find a town where there's more love than in the town of Miracle.

MY CHRISTMAS PRAYER

Dearest God, please never let me
Crowd my life full to the brim.
So like the keeper of Bethlehem's
  inn,
I find I have no room for Him.

Instead, let my heart's door be
  ever open,
Ready to welcome the newborn
  King,
Let me offer the best I have,
To Him who gives me **everything.**

ROSALYN HART FINCH

THE EMPTY MANGER

Drue Duke

It was the Saturday night dress rehearsal of the Christmas pageant to be presented at the worship service the next night. I sat on one of the folding chairs which had been set up in the fellowship hall of our church, sulking. **I should be up on that stage in the role of Mary,** I fumed. Never in my entire sixteen years had I been more amazed than when Mr. Elliott, who was in charge, announced that Eloise would have the role. Why, I was experienced. I'd been in every pageant that church ever had.

"We're using some fresh, new actors," Mr. Elliott explained when I questioned his choice. "But I'm counting on you to help backstage."

So that's how I got stuck with the job of property chairman, rounding up all that stuff they use on the stage, like the manger and hay and a doll to represent the Baby Jesus.

I watched the action. Now the shepherds were coming in. Eloise leaned down to pick up the Baby out of the manger. She stopped, looked confused, whispered something to the boy playing Joseph. He looked into the manger and shrugged.

Mr. Elliott's voice rang from the back of the room, "What's the problem?"

"There's no baby in here," Eloise answered.

I heard my name shouted, but I was already on my feet, headed for the door that led backstage. There, in the wings, in a box, lay the stuffed doll, just where I had left it.

I ran onto the stage, laid the doll in the manger and shrunk out as fast as I could through the nearest stage exit. I hid in the wings as I heard Mr. Elliott call, "Is everything set now? Good. Let's go on."

The pageant continued without further interruption, and as soon as all of the cast cleared the stage I hurried on to gather up the props. I hoped to get through and leave before anyone could say anything about my mistake. But I was not quick

enough. Mr. Elliott came on the stage, and as I reached for the doll, he said, "Wait just a minute. Let's talk."

I was certain he was going to scold me, and I stiffened to ward off his angry words. Instead, his voice was very soft.

"You didn't like serving as property chairman, did you?" he asked.

I only shook my lowered head to indicate that indeed I did not like the job.

"In fact, you rather resented it, didn't you?"

I either had to admit that, which I didn't relish doing, or lie about it. So I said nothing.

"I didn't choose you to play Mary," he said, "because you don't need the experience. You are not shy like Eloise. She needs to learn to get up in front of people, and I want to help her. I needed someone to handle all the miscellaneous things to outfit the stage, someone I could depend on. I thought I had that someone in you."

I felt tears welling up in my eyes.

"I'm sorry I failed you," I muttered.

"No, my dear," he said, "it wasn't I whom you failed." He squatted down beside the manger which still held the doll. "Look at this," he said. "Do you see what you left out?"

I looked at the doll, then at him.

"This doll represents the Lord Jesus in this pageant," he said. "Doesn't that say something to you?"

I knew at once what he meant. I nodded, and he waited for me to speak.

"When I get angry or jealous," I said slowly, "I might leave Jesus out?"

"When you get angry or jealous," he amended, "you are **sure** to leave Jesus out. Out of your plans, out of your life, out of your heart. Don't forget that."

I picked the doll up and held it close to me.

"I won't forget," I said.

And I was sure I never would.

THE FIRST GIFT EXCHANGE

June Masters Bacher

The little grey bird was growing tired. This was his first flight south to escape the bitter cold and his untried wings were weary. Dare he rest again? Yielding to an earlier temptation to rest was the reason he became separated from the flock. "I must go on," he told himself, remembering his mother's teaching, "lest the star should set before I find my way."

Flying alone against the star-struck sky gave him time to ponder the vastness of the universe—so different from the security of his down-lined nest. Weren't there more stars than he remembered seeing through the branches of his first home? Why was the one he followed so brilliant? Why did some of the other birds he had seen along the way to Judaea have such beautiful songs while he had only a wee chirp? And why were some so brightly-feathered while neither his breast nor his wings were touched with color? "I wish," he told the ever-larger star, "that I were beautiful—I wish my wings were strong. Maybe I will never reach my destination."

Down, down went the star—and then it seemed to stop. Could this be a sign that he, too, was to descend? Even as he hesitated, the little bird saw movement below. With a chirp of joy, he dropped to the earth. There he crouched, resting and listening for familiar bird-voices. But the sounds he heard were unfamiliar: a comforting "Moo," a sleepy "Ba-a-a," and the soft "Coos" of some strange bird.

Hopping to the nearby building, he peered inside and there saw a strange sight in the glow of a low-burning fire. A tiny baby, wrapped only in loose garments, lay partly exposed in the manger while the mother slept on the hay and the father dozed near the fire.

He had heard fire was important to people. For with no wings they couldn't follow the sun as birds did. The man should be tending the fire. If it went out, wouldn't the baby be cold or die?

"Wake up! Wake up!" The little bird tried to rouse the father, first with a chirp

and then with a little tug on his mantel with his beak. There was no response from the sleeping man, but a low cry from the baby. Maybe he was uncovered.

As the bird flew over the dying embers he felt their warmth and saw to his surprise that the movement of his own wings had fanned life back into them. And then he knew what he must do.

All night he flew back and forth, back and forth. The embers burned lower with each flight and sometimes it was necessary to fly very close to fan any life into them at all. Often he felt uncomfortably warm and knew he was dangerously near the fire. But one thought remained. He must keep it burning to keep the baby warm.

As the first fingers of dawn reached through the cracks of the crude building, the little bird realized that he was too exhausted to continue his vigil. With a sad chirp of despair, he fell wearily at the feet of the father.

The man stirred, and picked up the fallen bird. "This little creature kept the fire going," he said. Joseph checked on the baby, cozy and warm, touched the

cheek of his wife tenderly, and then warmed the bird with his cupped hands. When he felt a stir of life, Joseph put down a few crumbs from last night's meager meal and poured water from an earthen pitcher.

As the bird bent his head to drink, something wonderful happened to his small breast. It turned brick-red—and beautiful!

"Thank you and thank you!" the little robin tried to chirp, but it wasn't a chirp anymore. The sound Joseph and Mary heard as he spread his strong new wings was a song, a carol, that echoed long after he had disappeared in the heavens. "Peace on earth . . ." it seemed to be saying again to the shepherds in the hills.

AFTER-CHRISTMAS PRESENTS

Laura Norman

It is June. Outside the flowers are blooming, the sun is shining, and I am enjoying a Christmas present.

Last summer, Danny, the little boy from down the street, asked if he could mow my lawn for two dollars.

Poor little guy, I thought, **probably trying to earn a little money.** He would have no way of knowing how small a retired teacher's check could be in these days in inflation.

My yard is small. I could mow it myself. And two dollars was more than I could really afford. I had to turn him down.

Then came fall and the winter snow, and the lawn was forgotten.

Christmas Eve I was hanging a wreath on my door when Danny came again.

"Well now," I said, smiling at him, "I do not believe the lawn needs mowing today."

"I brought you a Christmas present," he said, handing me an envelope. Then looking a little embarrassed he quickly said goodbye.

I opened the letter and I shall never forget the contents, written in a childish hand.

Dear neighbor:
I have a present for you. Next summer I will mow your lawn all summer. Merry Christmas.

Danny

Danny has done far more than mow my lawn this summer. He has taught me that the gift worth giving is the gift of self. This Christmas I will have gifts for **my** neighbors, little favors that I can do for them throughout the year.

I hope, like me, they will all be enjoying my Christmas gifts when flowers are blooming and the sun is shining.

LOVE CAME DOWN
AT CHRISTMAS

Love came down at Christmas,
Love all lovely, love divine.
Love was born at Christmas,
Star and angels gave the sign.

Love shall be our token,
Love be yours and love be mine.
Love to God and all men,
Love shall be our gift and sign.

SILENT NIGHT

Nancy Schraffenberger

They had planned it for weeks, with care and concern.

Not a single loved person or Christmas amenity was missing from Frederick Bonnerman's house on the night of December 24th. The scene was as perfect as a stage setting. But the minute his wife Carrie rolled his chair into the middle of the living room, he felt more than ever like a great wooden puppet.

All of his children and their wives and husbands were there, along with every one of the grandchildren—from dark-haired Stephen, on the threshold of young manhood at age thirteen, to small Amy, the five-year-old, a Christmas bonbon in her rose-pink dress. The spicy tang of bayberry candles, burning applewood logs and pine scented the air. In the corner, a towering evergreen glowed with its multi-colored lights and ornaments. The sideboard was laid with a buffet service of

87

the best silver and crystal, pastel china and snowy linen, and, nearby, a tea table held eggnog, mulled cider, miniature sandwiches and cookies.

The old man looked at it all stonily then shifted his large frame to a more militarily erect position. His blunt lionlike features were still handsome at seventy-three, and he was dressed in the same green velvet jacket he'd always worn just for the holidays. But this time, for him, it was a charade, not a celebration. He'd bristled with annoyance when Carrie pinned a badge of bright crimson holly berries on his lapel, as if he were some sort of grand marshal. But she'd only smiled and, as she did every Christmas, had given him the small pottery figure to hold. He rolled it back and forth as he cupped it in his good left hand, the chipped and blurred figure of a sleeping Baby.

Now, one by one, the members of Frederick Bonnerman's family began approaching him, their faces expectant. Christmas had always been such a special time and they clearly hoped that this painstakingly wrought celebration would cheer him. But he fended them off with an icy blue stare, chilling their soft greetings with his silence. He knew he was spoiling it for them. He couldn't help himself. And that was the crux of it.

The stroke a few months earlier had left his speech garbled and his muscles uncooperative. And now he couldn't take care of the necessary tasks, couldn't feed himself or dress or keep himself clean without help.

Frederick Bonnerman was not a complaining man and not a self-pitying one either. He was too proud for that; his life, all-told, had been too fortunate to be whining about a few latter-day physical defects. So when the numbness had taken over his body, he had invited it into his spirit as well.

Behind his chair, he could hear Amy's voice, "Why doesn't Grandpa like me to pet him anymore?" and her mother hushing her. "Grandpa's been very sick. He's just tired, honey."

His lips trembled, and he pressed them into a stern, straight line.

Trying to make the best of the evening,

his oldest daughter, Emily, started to play some carols on the piano. The grownups and children clustered around her, singing softly, aware of the heavy silence from the center of the room. Carrie sat beside him, her warm hand resting on top of his cold one, her light, sweet voice distinct among the singers. He shifted impatiently in his chair and she leaned close. "It'll be time to start the Bible reading in a few minutes. You're not getting too tired, are you, Frederick?"

He shook his head curtly, his eyes turning to the low table in front of the fireplace. There lay the family's Christmas treasure—century-old, handmade clay figures arranged in the familiar crèche grouping, except for the Baby he held in his hand. After the older children had taken turns reading the nativity Scriptures, the youngest, Amy, would put the Child in the manger. Exactly at midnight. Exactly as the Bonnerman children had done for three generations.

The old man's eyes rested on the figures: Mary and Joseph, the Wise Men, a shepherd, an ox and a lamb—their colors muted with age, the shapes nicked and worn. Frederick Bonnerman's own grandfather, a farmer and amateur potter, had formed them, not with great skill, but with an appealing, primitive simplicity—the work of a grown-up molding clay with the joy and freedom of a child. Much cherished, carefully preserved, they'd been passed from father to son, father to son, and every Bonnerman child's understanding of Christmas began with these old figures. It seemed, to Frederick Bonnerman, these were the only precious things he had left to give his family.

The mantel clock chimed 11:30, its mellow belltones mingling with the last notes of "It Came Upon a Midnight Clear." Emily turned to her father from the piano bench, eyebrows questioning. He nodded. They would begin.

Slowly, everyone gathered around the table, with Frederick's wheelchair at one end. Stephen opened the Bible to the chapter marked with a faded blue satin ribbon. He cleared his throat and began to read in his boy's cracking tenor: "And it came to pass in those days, that there

went out a decree from Caesar Augustus . . ."

Stephen handed the book to his sister and she to the next oldest child until each had read—except for Amy, who would take the Baby to the manger.

The clock was striking twelve times as she came toward Frederick, sturdy as a cub, her silky brown hair cut like a close-fitting cap around her small head. Her little round face wore a serious expression, but her eyes danced with excitement and pride as they gazed into her grandfather's. Tenderly she lifted the tiny Baby cupped in his hand, turned in a whirl of rose-pink ruffles and stepped away from him toward the manger on the table. Then it happened.

One of Amy's feet twisted and she tumbled down like a dropped ragdoll, her arms flinging out, the clay Baby falling on the slate hearth with a small tinkling sound, the awful sound of breaking.

Amy's face broke too. He saw the look of happiness shatter. She turned to him. Everyone did. And then Stephen's voice interrupted the frozen moment. "Oh, please, Grandpa, please don't be mad . . .

because we can still keep Him, can't we?"

He looked at the sad faces surrounding him. They looked back. And saw.

Of course, Frederick Bonnerman could not speak. But words weren't necessary, for a great warmth was rising in him, like a sun, up from his feet through all of his body until his eyes shone with the brightness of it and the expression on his face was speech itself.

His face said that whatever Frederick Bonnerman could not do, he was still able to understand, comfort, love and forgive.

For the space of a breath no one moved, and them it seemed to Frederick Bonnerman that no one was **not** moving. Hands were picking Amy up and arms were enfolding her and other hands were carefully recovering the broken pieces of pottery. And arms, many arms, were around the old man's shoulders. And with his good left hand he was reaching out to Amy.

For Frederick Bonnerman and his family, the Christ Child had truly wholly come.

PART IV
Christmas Memories

GRAMMY'S CRÈCHE

Elaine St. Johns

The Grammy who started it all was my mother, Adela Rogers St. Johns. It was after I moved to California with my two-year-old daughter, Kristen and six-year-old son, George. We all lived together, along with an aunt and uncle and various friends and relations, in a family compound called **The Hill.**

As Christmas approached, Grammy decided more than one Christmas tree was redundant, so for her house she bought, instead, a sturdy, rustic, peak-roofed shed, charming Mary and Joseph figurines, a small wooden manger, and of course the Royal Infant Himself. The whole was set up on a living room table surrounded with holiday greens and poinsettias. (The Infant hidden snugly out of sight until Christmas Eve.) The children thought the very merry Christmas tree at our house was for "pretty"; but at Grammy's house, where we gathered together on Christmas Eve, and Baby Jesus appeared in the manger, Grammy's crèche,

though simple, was the focus of reverence and awe.

Small wonder that Kristen and George started to save from their pocket money to add to Grammy's crèche. On those long-ago Christmas Eves, as we read the Christmas story from the Gospels, the children would present their gifts. One year an exotic Wise Man; another, four tiny shepherds and one too-large sheep; then a blue ceramic donkey, a plump porcelain angel with a rose atop her head . . .

The children grew up, married and moved away. Grammy's work as a writer led her to move permanently to a hotel in New York. **The Hill** was no more and the crèche went into storage.

Then my granddaughter was born. It was just before Jessica's first Christmas that a large package was delivered to me from the storage warehouse. The card read, "From one grandmother to another." It was Grammy's crèche. And there they were—Mary and Joseph and Jesus, the Wise Man, the big sheep and too-small shepherds, the blue donkey minus one ear, the angel **sans** rose, but what matter? I carefully set the scene on a table in the living room. After all, more than one Christmas tree is redundant!

It was before this manger that Jessica and later her brother Bogart learned the blessed Christmas story and the beloved carols. And then these two began to bring gifts to the stable. An early offering was a tiny gift-wrapped package of peanuts. Later, with allowances hoarded throughout December, Christmas by Christmas, arrived a variety of angels, several deer, a cow, and more odd sheep. Not quite every beast of the field nor all the great sea monsters gathered before the Holy Family, but there did appear a white horse, an otter, a lion, a handsome orangutan, Jonah's whale and, since Bo found out what Behemoth meant, a hippopotamus.

Grammy's crèche became a neighborhood attraction, with all the children dropping by each year during Christmas week to watch it grow.

Two years ago, Jessica and Bo made an Advent wreath to place at the manger site, and each of the four Sundays before Christmas we ceremoniously lighted a candle and sang carols. This past year they arranged the scene themselves, using my brick fireplace with its raised hearth. Books, stacked to form a series of gentle terraces to the hearth, were covered with a white sheet and cotton snow, sure footing for men and beasts. The fireplace was filled with pine boughs from their yard, and on the hearth itself was the crèche with its familiar, well-loved figures.

On Christmas Eve, as Jessica, now ten, placed the Infant in His manger and her mother, father, Bo and I sang one last "Silent Night," I inwardly thanked my mom for her gift. Not only for the tangible objects themselves but for her gift of wisdom in establishing a tradition that strengthens our family and its sense of continuity. For one day, I know, in the not-too-distant future, I will give my daughter Grammy's crèche: "From one grandmother to another."

THE CHESS PIE CHRISTMAS

Doris Davis Engles

It wasn't my first depression Christmas, but it was the one that at age nine would forever change the way I believed Christmas should be. Our family was always together at Grandma's, but most of the preparations were complete by the time we arrived from Pittsburgh.

The one task left was the making of chess pies. These were individual pies that Grandma baked with extra love and care for our family and some of Grandma's special friends in the little town where she lived. So this was the Christmas event we always did together.

I watched as Grandma rolled out the dough.

"How many will we be giving away this year, Grandma?" I asked, wondering if I might have more than one for myself.

"Well, there's Uncle Zeke who lives alone, and the Evans sisters who have no other relatives to share Christmas with them. Then there's Aunt Emma who asks never to be left out of my Christmas pie list. Oh, yes, there's Mrs. Goldstein who's blind and lives alone. We mustn't ever forget her. You remember we went to see her last summer when you were here?"

I shivered as I thought about the dark old living room with its massive wall paintings and velvet sofa with claw feet that I felt might move at any moment. I hoped I wouldn't have to go there with the chess pies.

At last they were done. We would deliver them the afternoon before Christmas, but for now they must be put out of sight to be safe.

"Here, on the top shelf of this cupboard should be a safe place, and out of the way, too," she said. "I don't use it much."

The next afternoon we cleaned off the

95

kitchen table to prepare the chess pies for delivery. Grandfather would drive us to Uncle Zeke's and Aunt Emma's. Then we'd go on to the Evans sisters' home where they would squeeze a nickel into my hand as we prepared to leave. Finally, near suppertime my job was to go to Mrs. Goldstein's since she lived the closest to Grandma's house.

The trays were on the table now ready to uncover. I couldn't wait to taste that brown sugary sauce, heavy with chopped nuts and raisins. I had decided to eat one of mine before we made our deliveries. Grandma peeled back the wax paper on the first tray and we both stared in amazement. She said nothing, but her shocked face was white.

"Oh Grandma, what's happened?" Bits of crust lay on the tray edges and there were holes in every pie. Quickly Grandma pulled the wax paper from the second tray. I felt relieved the minute I saw the pies. They were perfect. Nothing had bothered them.

"It must have been a mouse," she said thoughtfully. "That cupboard hasn't been used much for sometime. As least we have one tray left. As I see it we'll have just enough to give as gifts."

"Oh no, Grandma! You mean that we're not going to keep any for ourselves?"

"Dear, it would be so easy to keep them for ourselves. But Christmas means giving."

Why did that mouse spoil everything? All I wanted was one pie. Somehow this kind of giving wasn't what I'd expected of Christmas.

The disappointment I was feeling was still evident when I reached Mrs. Goldstein's big brick house with the huge windowed sunporch. I slipped inside and knocked at the inner door. It was dark and bare. No Christmas decorations appeared anywhere. Mrs. Goldstein opened the door just enough to ask who was there.

"I'm Doris, Mrs. Port's granddaughter," I mumbled. "I've brought you something for Christmas from my Grandmother."

"Come in, do come in, dear," she said loudly. She motioned me to a chair with her cane. I slipped into the seat covered with needlepoint and sat back in the cool dimness. My feet hung loosely above the soft carpeting, and I waited silently until Mrs. Goldstein seated herself nearby.

"Did you and your Grandmother bake those wonderful chess pies this year?" she asked smiling. "I always look forward to her thoughtfulness. It's really the only gift I'm given except from my family. And they're all gone from home now." I squirmed uneasily in the chair. She was going to have my chess pies.

"Yes, we made them yesterday. Grandma always waits until I come for Christmas before she bakes, because she knows how much I like them," I answered.

"Wait here," she said as she moved to the edge of her chair and then rose on her cane.

She tapped effortlessly across the room and disappeared through the hallway into the kitchen.

In a moment she returned, carrying a cardboard box lined with Christmas paper.

"This is for you, Doris. Since you delivered my gift, I want you to have this from me. I hope you like oranges and candy."

I took the box carefully from her outstretched hand.

"The fruit is from my son in Florida and the candy is from my daughter in New York. Merry Christmas and I know God has blessed you."

She was still smiling out into the darkness as I stepped on the sunporch and into the street beyond. Trudging along in the deeper snow I saw out of the growing darkness tiny new flakes drifting toward the ground. Lights in nearby houses were on now, and the brilliant color of Christmas trees flooded the windows. My fingers touched the edges of the wonderful candies under the paper covering, and I could smell the sweet fragrance of the oranges.

Somewhere down the block I heard sounds of "Silent Night" being sung by early carolers. Suddenly I knew the chess pies didn't matter. What mattered was having something to give.

Opening the door with one hand and waving the gift box with the other, I called excitedly, "Grandma, you'll never guess what happened!"

NO FAMILY FOR CHRISTMAS

Marilyn Morgan Helleberg

"**I** don't think we'll bother with a tree this year," said my mother. "It doesn't seem right to celebrate. Besides, my heart just wouldn't be in it."

"No tree?" I choked back tears. It was 1943, and my father was on a ship somewhere in the South Pacific. We'd had no mail from him for several weeks (though he and Mom wrote every day), so we weren't even sure he was still alive. My brother was in Navy boot camp and wouldn't be home for Christmas either, so Mom and I would be alone in the house, except for the young Army couple we'd rented the basement to.

The thought of such a maimed Christmas pressed on my heart like a rock. The weeks crept slowly by with none of the joyful expectancy that would have normally brightened our household as Christmas drew near. Mother had erected a cold, gray wall around her—there were no tears, no self-pity, just a rigid, distant stoicism that made me feel lost and scared. I even remember tiptoeing around the house as if to be invisible, so I wouldn't intrude on the pain that imprisoned her.

About a half hour after Mother had announced her decision, there was a knock at our kitchen door. Ruthann, the wife of the young soldier we'd rented our basement to, stood there crying.

"Jim's being sent overseas the day after Christmas." Uninvited, Ruthann suddenly threw her arms around Mother and sobbed against her shoulder, and as I watched I could actually see Mother's stiff body begin to soften. Then, incredibly, Mother's own tears began to come

. . . slowly at first, then in great body-wracking sobs. The two of them stood there crying out their loneliness. I felt strangely relieved . . . lifted . . . free.

"God bless you," said Ruthann, as she pulled a hanky from her apron pocket and dried her eyes. Then Mother reached over, pulled me close to her, and with one arm around me and the other around Ruthann, she said, "And God bless you . . . both of you."

Ruthann started back down the stairs.

"Ruthann," Mom called after her, "why don't you and Jim come up for a while after supper tonight? Marilyn and I were just getting ready to go buy our Christmas tree, and we'd sure like to have you two help us trim it."

THE FOURTH WISE MAN

Linn Ann Huntington

Looking back, I can't recall exactly who thought up the idea for the practical joke on Richie. Maybe it was Jimmy Ray or Ben. Maybe I did. It was one week after our team, the Blue Raiders, had lost the 8th grade district football title. And there was no doubt in any of our minds as to whose fault that was—Richie's.

I don't know when I first realized Richie wasn't quite like everyone else. He was a year older than the rest of us, having been held back a grade. He was a big kid who walked awkwardly and spoke haltingly.

We were behind by three points when Richie came into that game. He broke through their defensive line with no trouble at all. Jimmy Ray lofted a perfect pass and Richie stood there in the middle of the field and pulled it in. The crowd went wild, screaming "Go, Go." And maybe that's why it happened. In all the noise, Richie became confused and ran the

wrong way. It was a 46-yard touchdown pass and Richie had scored six points for the **other** team.

So that's how we came to think up the joke on Richie. Every year on the day before Christmas vacation our homeroom had a Christmas party in the afternoon and the traditional pageant for our families that night. We all drew names from a box and bought an inexpensive gift for that person to exchange at the party. I drew Richie's name and Jimmy Ray and Ben and I knew just what we'd get him. It was more expensive than the usual things but we pooled our money. The joke on big, slow Richie was worth it.

As we nibbled the cookies and sipped the punch the PTA provided, we could hardly wait for the gift opening. Finally our teacher, Mrs. Marlowe, announced that it was time for Santa's arrival. The principal, dressed in a Santa suit, came running in with a lot of "Ho, ho, ho's" and started picking up the packages under the tree and calling out the names. There were the usual scarves, records and other stuff that each kid knew the other had wanted. We knew Richie wanted the gift we had for him but he was in for a real surprise.

Finally Richie's name was called. I held my breath as he fumbled with the ribbons and paper. Then he pulled out a football. Ben had painted it a garish purple, intended to resemble our school color. The inscription in bold red letters said mockingly, "OUR HERO."

The cafeteria grew quiet. Mrs. Marlowe turned around, her face angry. Her eyes searched the room and rested on the three of us. I was trying hard to keep a straight face but in that instant I knew **she** knew. And I also knew we were in for big trouble.

Richie just stood there in the middle of the room, his mouth open. He gently stroked the football, his eyes blinking behind thick glasses.

I tried to duck out of school as soon as the party was over, but Mrs. Marlowe stopped me. "I want to talk to you, Carl. Why did you do it?"

"It was just a joke," I mumbled, wish-

ing I could fall through the floor.

"A joke!" She paused. "We'll talk about this later. I don't have time right now, but I want to see you backstage after tonight's program. Understood?" I nodded.

The Christmas pageant helped take my mind off my own problems. The Glee Club sang Christmas carols during the set changes, the candles they held flickering softly in the auditorium. From the elevated cage where I worked the lights I had a good view of the stage. Now my spotlight focused on the one single large star near the top of the backdrop. I could almost visualize how it must have been on that night long ago, how vast the sky must have looked to those shepherds tending their flocks outside Bethlehem.

Then the narrator's voice was saying, "And suddenly there was with the angel a multitude of the Heavenly host, praising God and saying, 'Glory to God in the highest, and on earth peace, good will toward men.' "

Good will toward men. The words made me wince. Mrs. Marlowe's eye caught mine and I wished I'd never seen or heard of that stupid football.

I asked one of the other guys to take over for me and I hurried toward the dressing rooms. I found Richie sitting alone in one corner, dressed as a wise man, the football in his hands.

I stood before him, hands sunk in my pockets and took a deep breath. "Richie, I'm sorry. I was the one who gave you the football."

He looked up. "**You** gave me the football, Carl?" I nodded, my face feeling flushed. "It must have been awfully expensive, Carl. I always wanted a football. You're a good guy, Carl." Richie's face lit up and he smiled a wide smile at me.

I started to speak but suddenly he heard his cue and he hurried up to the stage. From the wings, I watched the

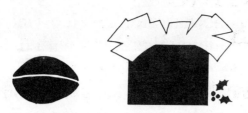

three Wise Men make their way on stage. The first two in turn presented their gifts of gold and frankinscense. Then it was Richie's turn. Carefully he stepped to the manger.

"This gift I bring to the baby Jesus," he began. Then he paused. The crowd stirred uneasily. "This gift I bring to the baby Jesus," he began again. And from the folds of his robe he withdrew the gift. But it wasn't the expected flask of myrrh. I gasped along with the audience as Richie held up his purple football.

"I've always wanted a football of my very own," he said quietly to the doll inside the manger. "My friend Carl got me this one." He looked out to the audience. "This football means a lot to me," he stammered. "But I want to give it to the Baby Jesus." Gently he laid the ball in the manger.

The auditorium was silent as the curtain closed. Then the audience exploded into applause. Richie came up to me, his fake beard slightly askew. "You don't mind that I gave the football away, do you Carl?"

I shook my head, trying to dislodge the lump in my throat.

"Carl, those words on the football. What did that one word say—H-E-R-O. What does that mean?"

I struggled to find the right words. "A hero is someone everybody looks up to."

He looked surprise. "Does everyone look up to me, Carl?"

I put my hand to his shoulder, then helped him straighten his crooked beard. "Yes, Richie, tonight you're everyone's hero. Just listen to that crowd. They're applauding you.

He listened and his face broke into a wide grin. I pushed him on stage for his curtain call. Mrs. Marlowe came and stood beside me.

"I heard what you told Richie," she said, smiling at me. "I think he was probably the wisest of our three Wise Men tonight. But you know," she added, smiling at me." I think maybe now there's a fourth one."

A CANDLELIGHTING CHRISTMAS

Virginia Westevelt

Candlelighting time in our home begins at bedtime on Christmas Eve. The children have trimmed the tree, the stockings have been hung, and the children are ready for bed. They stand, their eyes shining with excitement, while the room is darkened. Then, like a touch of magic, the Christmas tree sparkles to life. It is the signal for our Candlelighting ceremony to begin.

First, a tall candle is placed in the living room window, its tip aglow, "to light the Christ Child on his way." Its flickering rays pick out the crèche from the shadows and softly highlight the mother and cradle.

Two pajama-clad figures, Dirck, six, and Deidre, four and one-half, stand near, each with a small candle. "Now?" asks Dirck eagerly, and he tilts his tiny candle toward the tall taper. Turning, he lights his sister's candle from his. Then, while we sing "Silent Night," the children go slowly up the stairs, candles gleaming against the darkness.

Christmas will always be for them . . . voices singing, "Sleep in heavenly peace" . . . tiny candles flickering in the dark . . . and the love of Christ radiating His beaming light into the world.

THE ROOFTOP CHRISTMAS

Marjorie Holmes

It would be our first Christmas in the huge Victorian house we'd bought in Washington, D.C. "And now that we've got it painted inside and out," said my husband Lynn, "let's decorate the outside from stem to stern for Christmas!"

I groaned. "Honey, I'm tired. Let's wait another year." All summer and well into the fall I'd been scraping, sanding, painting. The house had been in terrible condition; but it was cheap and enormous, on a big shady corner lot, next door to the Episcopal church and across the street from school. It was a lot of work, but well worth the effort. And now that the renovations were done, I didn't want to look at another paint brush or hammer or sandscraper.

Lynn looked crestfallen. However, I listened dutifully to his plans. "We can outline the gingerbready roofs, cupolas and porches with colored lights . . . put up some silhouettes," he said thoughtfully. "I found some old linoleum rugs in the attic, and all you have to do," he assured me, "is draw the figures on them." I still wasn't convinced.

"Make Santa and his reindeer!" our six-year-old chimed in.

"No," my husband said firmly. "I think Christmas should be Christian." He turned to me. "Don't you?" Then, ignoring my silence, "How about some Wise Men riding camels? . . . Look, I'll cut them out and set them up; it shouldn't be much work for you at all. Of course, if you really **mind**. . . ."

I did. Art had been my second major in college; it shouldn't be too hard just to **draw** the things. But I knew from experience how impossible it would be to keep from getting involved. And I was indeed tired—Christmas or not. Meanwhile, the family eagerly went trooping to the attic to undertake the project without me. I hated myself for being a killjoy. "Well, **I** can draw pretty good," one child was saying.

I just couldn't stand it. I got up and

went trudging after them.

They were already unrolling and measuring the stiff, worn rugs. Quietly I slipped into a corner and sat down with a bunch of old Christmas cards, looking for models, ideas. The unfinished wood of the attic smelled sweet—like a barn—and gradually a tender excitement began to build in me, the first stirrings of the Christmas spirit.

"Okay," I called, "how big do you want your camels?"

They turned in surprise and came running to hug me. "Life-size," my husband said. "It's a big roof."

Before the day was over, I had roughed out patterns on long rolls of wrapping paper. Lynn cut out the figures with a linoleum knife, and braced them, dark side out, with pieces of lath. By nightfall, backed by amber lights, three Wise Men rode in silent splendor toward the scalloped balcony at the front of the house. . . . **The perfect place for a manger scene** I realized as I looked up awed at what we had wrought.

Now it was my husband who protested. "Hey, that'll mean more rugs."

"Then find them," I laughed.

And he did—he and the boys—at a second-hand store.

So, next was Mary and Joseph, bent in tender silhouette above their baby in the manger. And we couldn't stop now—we had to have the shepherds, too, on another rooftop, leading or carrying their sheep toward the miracle the angels had promised.

And oh, how beautiful it was when it was finally finished. You could see them for blocks . . . the silent, radiant figures telling again the story of God's love for the world. I'll never forget how the church bells called us to midnight services that first Christmas Eve in Washington. And how people were drawn to our house afterward, inspired by that majestic rooftop Christmas scene. Some even came up the steps and joined us for coffee. New friends were made. Strangers driving by noticed it and told others. People across the city made pilgrimages to see it.

It became a tradition. Every year people looked for our rooftop pageantry. Occasionally they stopped, or telephoned or wrote us letters.

"Hey, Mom, this is wonderful," said my son, now a teen-ager. He read aloud to me one of a stack of letters we had just received.

"I'm a cocktail waitress. I have to work on Christmas Eve. But driving to and from work I go a few blocks out of my way to see your display. I can't say I'm a believer, but at Christmas when I see your house, I feel so good. And driving home after work, even if your lights are out, I still know they're there. It's sort of like they're watching over me. Well, I just want you to know and to say thank you."

My son grinned at me. "And to think you didn't even want to do it."

"Good heavens, do you remember that? It was years ago."

"I don't think any of us will ever forget, Mom. And when I'm married and have a family I hope I find a house with an attic and old linoleum rugs!"

"I hope so, too," I told him. And thinking back to that long-ago afternoon in the attic, I said, "and I hope your reluctant family member can discover the joy that I have."

For I know now that the symbols of Christmas are so much more than decoration. They can be shining strands that bind a family close. They can be the chain of continuity for future families. And, illumined, God Himself sometimes uses them to light the way for strangers.

THE GIFT THAT KEPT GIVING

Marion Bond West

Eleven years ago, on Christmas Eve, our little girls gave us a unique gift—so unique that it keeps on giving, year after year.

Julie and Jennifer were 6 and 8. Our twin sons, Jon and Jeremy were not yet 2. I remember I was tired. The boys had required constant attention. Still, I'd done all the things that I always did at Christmas. The tall tree was decorated, the gifts elaborately wrapped. The cooking was done. The door was decorated. Presents for the children had been carefully selected.

I was tired but happy. Julie stopped me in the kitchen. "Mama, Jennifer and I have a present for you and Daddy. It's not something you can wrap up. We want you and Daddy to sit on the sofa and hold the boys, so we can give it to you." I had a few more last-minute things to do, and I really didn't want to sit just then. "Please, Mama," Julie pleaded, "it'll only take a few minutes." I relented and called my husband. It took some doing to get the boys settled in our laps. Finally, though, we were ready for the gift. Julie and Jennifer stood nervously on the hearth, holding hands. They wore red flannel granny gowns with little matching dust caps. "First, we have to turn out the lights," Julie said in a hushed voice. "We just want the Christmas lights from the tree to shine," Jennifer explained.

IT DIDN'T SEEM LIKE CHRISTMAS!

Jeff Japinga

Oh, yes, the little angel stood gracefully at the top of the tree as she had for each of my nineteen Christmases, her skirt a little grayer, perhaps, but after all, it's tradition she be there.

But she wasn't enough to make it feel like Christmas. College pressures—final examinations, especially—had demanded my full attention. Now, just a few days before Christmas, I had returned home. I had already missed out on so many of our traditions—the nightly lighting of the candles in an Advent wreath, the decorating of the tree, making a candy wreath for the front door . . .

So tonight, even caroling seemed out of place. A cold, penetrating drizzle fell, so foreign for this time of year when mounds of snow usually covered this part of Michigan. **How can it be Christmas when you can still see the grass?** I pouted. And I was depressed.

I hung to the back of our caroling group as we moved from house to house. I wanted to be happy, to tease the little children as we walked, to laugh joyously with the adults. But I didn't feel it . . . No, it didn't seem like Christmas. We were leaving the yard of one house when the lady called to me. "Young man," she said, "thank you so much for coming."

Looking straight ahead, they sang "Silent Night." Then Julie recited a poem about the love of God. After she finished, Julie asked her Daddy, shyly, "Will you please read us the Christmas story from the Bible, about Jesus getting born? Our Sunday school teacher read it last Sunday."

Jerry got his Bible and read the story, leaning toward the tree so he could see. We all listened. Even the twins were quiet and sat still. When he finished, Julie asked so softly we could barely hear her, "Now can we pray together?"

We'd never really had family devotions

and we weren't sure how to start the prayer. But, nevertheless, a little self-consciously, we prayed, each of us, one at a time. I knew then that something very special was happening to our family. From our daughters' gift, we had learned that we could pray together. So, through the years we continued having devotionals, not just at Christmas time, but all through the year.

Our little daughters' gift to the family, on that long-ago Christmas Eve, was the gift of faith. It has grown and supported our family ever since. It's a gift that keeps on giving.

"Oh, you're welcome," I said matter-of-factly.

"You know, I didn't feel much like celebrating this year," she continued. "All my family is gone now—all those things we used to do together. But you folks reminded me there are many ways of celebrating peace and love. Joy to the world, young man, the Lord has come!"

As I looked down the street at the rest of the group, I understood what she meant. People walked hand in hand; children excitedly chatted with each other. "Peace on earth, goodwill among men," was the silent message I saw.

I turned to the old woman. "Ma'am, I know how you feel. Merry Christmas!"

I sat up late that night at home, watching the warm glow of the light behind our Christmas angel. For years I had been the one to confirm the coming of Christmas by placing that angel at the top of the tree. But this year, that tradition was taken from me. A wonderful woman, an angel herself, showed me a new kind of Christmas . . . just a simple declaration: **The Lord has come.**

As I climbed the stairs to bed, I took one last look out the window. The light drizzle had turned into a soft snowfall. Yes, it really did seem like Christmas. **Joy to the World.**

THE CHRISTMAS IN MAMA'S KITCHEN

Jean Bell Mosley

For years, we put the Christmas tree in the parlor. It was the fanciest room in the old farmhouse—carpeted, wallpapered and curtained. It seemed fitting to celebrate the Master's birthday in the best room.

However, there was too much activity going on from day to day in the big kitchen—Mama's kitchen—to maintain an unused fire elsewhere, so there wasn't always a fire burning in the parlor. Grandma and Mama cooked, sewed, churned, washed and ironed in the kitchen. Dad and Grandpa kept their accounts, read the papers, soled shoes there. My two sisters and I did homework, helped with the chores, played our games there. Mama's kitchen fireplace was always aglow, the range constantly fired. It was a big spacious room—bright and cozy.

On December Sundays or special holidays, when company was expected, Dad would make a fire in the parlor stove and we'd all go in to enjoy the tree, breathe its cedary fragrance, touch the old familiar baubles. Baby Jesus, in his crib in the crèche beneath the tree, would, after a long time, feel warm to our touch.

But somehow the parlor never had the coziness Mama's kitchen had. I always liked the big center table we gathered around, face to face, making small talk or sometimes serious talk. If Mama read a Christmas story aloud in the parlor, it wasn't the same as in the kitchen accompanied by the sputtering fireplace and singing teakettle. Even our evening prayers seemed to come naturally in the kitchen.

One winter evening, as the fire died in the parlor stove, I boldly lifted the crib from the crèche and took it into the kitchen, setting it near the fireplace. My sisters, thinking I had been irreverent, told Mama.

"Let it be," Mama said. She smiled at

me, though I had expected a reprimand.

The next Christmas, when Dad and Grandpa brought the tree home, Mama said, "I mean to put it up here in the kitchen this year."

"Celebrate His birthday in here with the smell of cabbage cooking, the butter being churned, our old barn clothes hanging over there?" one of my sisters demanded.

"Let's try it," Mama said.

The hat rack was moved a little closer to the sewing machine. The cot was pushed up against another wall to make room. When we came downstairs for breakfast, in from the outdoor chores, home from school, there was the tree, bright, warm and fragrant. We trimmed it leisurely, cranberry chains one evening, popcorn garlands the next. Baby Jesus, in the crib, close and dear, was always warm, as were the little sheep, donkeys, shepherds and Wise Men.

When we read the Christmas story, starting seven nights before Christmas so each could have his turn at reading it, the event that happened so long ago and far away now seemed so close, as if it might have happened just last night in our own cow stable. I could visualize the Baby lying in Star's hay-lined feed box; hear the soft, velvety whinny of Dobbin looking on through the bars; the stirrings of other creatures that had come in from the cold.

The moon and stars that the shepherds saw that night in their pastures were the same moon and stars that shone on me when I went to close the chicken house door. White-bearded Grandpa, coming in from the snowy outdoors, bearing a gift of shiny red apples from the apple hole, looked very much like a Wise Man. We didn't know what had happened to our Christmas, but we knew it was better than any we'd ever had.

One afternoon a neighbor dropped in with some cookies. "Why, Myrtle," she said to Mama, "is this—is—this—appropriate—" Her voice trailed off. But after looking around the kitchen her face lit up. "Myrtle," she exclaimed, "you've brought Christmas in here to be an everyday thing, warm and comfortable, right amongst your living!"

Mama smiled and replied, "only our best for the Master." She may have winked at me. I don't know. Fireplace shadows sometimes play tricks, and holiday eyes get so bright they have to blink often.

MAKING ROOM FOR CHRISTMAS

Terri Castillo Uricolo

The subway car screeched to a halt and an unusually cheerful voice piped: "82nd Street, Jackson Heights—and Merry Christmas, everyone!" Wrapping my scarf around my neck, I stared at the happy faces glowing under the bright subway lights. Women and children clung excitedly to colorfully wrapped boxes tied with shiny ribbons. Men chatted merrily, exchanging holiday greetings. The festive scene was unlike the usual somber subway rides. Tonight was Christmas Eve and the air was electric. For everyone, that is, but me.

This was my first Christmas in New York City. Leaving my family and friends back in Hawaii, I had moved here several months earlier—a young woman curious about the "Big City." It promised to be an exciting life, but it was sometimes a lonely one, and making friends wasn't easy. I'd hoped to spend the holidays with another young woman I had met in my apartment building, but she had been unexpectedly called home for Christmas. Now, having no other friends living nearby, I would spend Christmas alone.

As happy spirits escalated around me, I felt more and more homesick. "This is supposed to be a family celebration," I kept telling myself. "How can I celebrate Christmas without my family?" All I could think of was the empty room waiting for me, the television set my only company.

I slushed through the buildup of snow on the subway platform and trudged down the icy steps leading to the street below. Strings of twinkling lights crisscrossed overhead along the avenue forming arches of stars against the dark night.

From the little shops lining the street, the sounds of Christmas carols floated through the air. I tucked my head under the hood of my coat to block out the sights and sounds around me. They only made me more homesick.

Light flurries of snow swirled against me as I quickened my pace. I'd soon be home. Crossing the street, I saw the big church on the corner. It was aglow with lots of candles burning brightly inside. A life-size crèche stood on the lawn with Joseph and Mary looking down at the Christ Child in the manger. A lighted sign next to it read: "Please join us for Midnight Mass on Christmas Eve." A tear slipped down my cheek. Midnight Mass was a tradition our family never missed. We **always** went to church **together** on Christmas Eve. To go without them would only add to the pain I already felt in being alone. "Why," I thought, "did I have to be 6,000 miles from home this night?"

Inside the entrance way to my building I fumbled for my keys. Then I heard it. A soft, vaguely familiar voice singing: "Joy to the world, the Lord is come . . ." I stopped and looked around. No one was there. I listened curiously. "Let earth receive her King . . ." I poked my head into the street. No one. I looked at the intercom unit on my right, and then I understood. The voice was coming from its speaker. Of course! It belonged to Mrs. Julia on the sixth floor, Mrs. Julia was a widow who lived alone in 6-B. She was a hearty soul who loved to stop residents in the lobby to chat—endlessly. More than once she'd told me more than I wanted to know about her herb garden and Felix, her house cat. Though she was a kind woman—she brought me chicken soup one afternoon when she heard I had the flu—I had been avoiding her recently. I knew she was lonely, but I just didn't have the time to listen to her non-stop chatter. Now, I could picture her sitting on the wooden stool next to the voice box in her kitchen, her wiry, silver hair tousled into a bun atop her head, singing to her neighbors as they came home.

As I listened my body lightened. Her voice rang out . . . "Let ev'ry heart . . . prepare Him room . . ." The words awak-

ened me like a splash of cold water on my face. **Prepare Him room** . . . "Why this is what Christmas is about," I thought, "preparing room for Christ in my heart." My mind raced back over the last few weeks. Had I prepared Him room? No, I hadn't. I had been too busy missing my family and friends. And in my loneliness I had **closed** my heart as tight as a clenched fist. To really celebrate Christmas meant I would have to **open** my heart—then I could make room for others. Maybe Christmas wouldn't have to be lonely after all.

Leaning against the intercom box, I drank in Mrs. Julia's radiant voice. "We wish you a Merry Christmas . . . we wish you a Merry Christmas . . ." she sang loudly. I pressed my finger on the button next to 6-B.

"Mrs. Julia," I said. "Mrs. Julia, this is Terri Castillo—down in 2-C."

"Merry Christmas, Terri!" she chimed back to me.

"Mrs. Julia," I asked as a smile crossed my face, "how would you like to go to Midnight Mass with me tonight?"

THE MAN IN THE RED BOUTONNIERE

James McDermott

New York is not an unfriendly town, yet, at Christmas time, when its legendary pace quickens, it makes some feel as if they've been left behind. At least that's the way I felt as my first Christmas in New York approached.

I was clinging to my first job as an assistant editor. The magazine I worked for was faltering; my editor spent most of his time on long telephone calls explaining why the rent hadn't been paid, and I spent most of my time wondering for how long I'd be paid.

So my steps were heavy as I trudged the forty blocks home through a late December drizzle to save the subway fare. My apartment was tucked far into the East Side in an old German neighborhood where the rents were still cheap, but tonight I walked north along Park Avenue thinking that its festively-planted center mall and richly-adorned apartment lobbies might give me a lift.

At about 70th Street, I noticed a lanky delivery boy teetering under the load of a huge carton. His only protection against the cold was a bright ski cap that was much too cheerful for his sad face. And the sleeves of a too-small stock clerk's gray cotton jacket hardly began to cover his gangling arms.

Just as we drew abreast, he turned to go in an apartment building, but he lost his balance, and the carton slid from his grasp, thudding sickeningly to the pavement. Instantly the cardboard darkened. With me hovering in helpless sympathy, the boy bent to open the box. Three of a dozen champagne bottles were smashed, frothing their extravagant contents on the rain-slicked sidewalk. "That's a week's work," he groaned. We looked at each other, and something deep inside each of us communicated the kind of hopelessness that the city of New York can make you feel when you have run your hardest and you know that it's not fast enough.

The doors to the apartment building whooshed open, and a dapper figure came between us. He was a small man, a derby perched jauntily on a thatch of white hair, and a red boutonniere tucked impeccably into his dark overcoat. He grasped us both by our elbows, drew us close to him and said in the low voice of a conspirator, "The French know a great deal about creating fine wine, but, as you two gentlemen are just discovering, they've never learned how to make a really good, durable bottle."

Perhaps for the first time that week, the delivery boy's face blossomed into a smile. And suddenly we, a curious threesome, were laughing aloud. But, just as suddenly, the little man interrupted us. "But, now, down to business." He turned to the boy. "Since I don't drink, these empty bottles here are of more use to me than your full ones. I'd like you to accept my payment for them right now."

The little man fetched two crisp bills from his wallet and tucked them deftly into the breast pocket of the boy's coat. Then, in a blink, he was gone.

I've never felt quite the same way about Christmas in New York since. And neither, I'm quite sure, has the boy in the bright ski cap.

MY VERY SPECIAL CHRISTMAS TREE

Madeline Weatherford

Christmas was the most special holiday of all for my father. The preparations, gift buying and decorations were no trouble to him and just added to his overall enjoyment.

I was introduced to my first Christmas tree when I was nine days old. Mother told me that it was a small tree but every ornament, candle and piece of silver tinsel were meticulously hung in place, as only he could do it. When he had finished, he took me from my bassinet and held me up to see his handiwork.

There were to be just four more of Daddy's Christmas trees—each one a little larger than the year before. And, of course, as I grew older his delight in Christmas rubbed off on me and it became my favorite holiday, too.

However, this year was going to be different. A short bout with pneumonia in February had snuffed out Daddy's life.

As Christmas drew near, Mother sat down with me and as gently as she could explained, "Madeline, we won't be able to have a tree and decorations this year because we're in mourning."

"In mourning" meant nothing to a four-going-on-five year old little girl. I missed my wonderful daddy and my once gay and beautiful mother, now weighed down by her grief.

Christmas Eve arrived with no special arrangements for the next day, other than early Mass and dinner with relatives. In the afternoon the phone rang and Mother answered.

"Oh, hello, Mrs. Dreyfus," she said. And after a pause, "That's very kind but I think we'll spend the evening here together. It's the first since—" She recovered and thanked Mrs. Dreyfus again and

hung up.

Mrs. Dreyfus was one of several Jewish families who lived in our apartment house. They had been wonderful to mother in helping her meet her sorrow and adjust to widowhood.

"What did she want?" I asked.

"She wanted us to come down this evening. I—I can't."

"Oh, please, Mother," I cried. "She always has hot cocoa for me."

Mother was silent most of the day and later in the evening she changed her mind. She called Mrs. Dreyfus and told her we'd stop in for a few minutes. "It's kind of her," Mother said, "and thank goodness they won't have any Christmas decorations."

We rang the doorbell and Mrs. Dreyfus welcomed us into the foyer. The living room beyond seemed dark with an odd-colored glow.

She led us into the living room where we were greeted with cries of "Merry Christmas." Seated around a beautifully decorated Christmas tree were Mrs. Abrams, Mrs. Cohen, Mrs. Blount. Under the tree were gaily decorated packages for us. And Mrs. Dreyfus didn't disappoint me. There was cocoa for me and coffee for the ladies.

There have been many, many trees since then—big, small, fresh and artificial—but I always think of that one as my very special Christmas tree. I'll never forget those loving, caring people who shared in an unfamiliar custom so that one little girl without a Daddy could have a Merry Christmas.

Today I can close my eyes and bring back that scene at will. Many times it has sustained me when things have gone badly; for I can still feel the warmth and love of those neighbors. It taught me the true meaning of Christmas—the brotherhood of man.

THE DOLL

Idella Bodie

"Mamma—" I pulled at my mother's skirt and pointed to the doll on the shelf of the department store. Mamma knew I had my heart set on a doll whose eyes would open and close.

It was 1933 and Christmas lay three weeks away. Mamma had taken us children on our annual trek from our quiet, rural home near Ridge Spring, South Carolina to the big, bustling city of Columbia to see the decorations and to tell Santa Claus we wanted black high-topped shoes and stockings for Christmas. It had been a hard year and money was scarce.

My father, a man of few words, had said "I doubt there'll be any toys in Santa's bag this year."

And Mamma had nodded in agreement, adding how lucky we were to live on a farm.

Careful to stay close to Mamma, I gazed in adoration at the doll. Her eyes were blue, and I could tell she would go to sleep when I laid her down. She had a rose bud of a mouth and a pale pink organdy dress and bonnet. I longed to hold her, but I was far too shy to ask.

In the following days—chilling winds sliced across our rolling farm, pushing us closer around the hickory fire. Cold gusts flickered the lamps as Daddy went in and out to do the chores; water froze in our wash basins. On long evenings I laid my head on our German shepherd and thought of the doll.

"Mamma," I'd try now and then. "I don't need any shoes. I want that doll." I could double the cardboard inside my shoe.

Always her answers were vague. Once I pressed her too far. "Oh," she said, "stop fretting. Santa may not make it at all this year."

When Christmas Eve finally came, I curled under the heaviness of the patchwork quilts, still yearning for the doll, and tried my best to lie still. As I asked God for the last time to let me have the doll, I remembered my Sunbeam leader, Miss Katie, and the stories she told us each Wednesday afternoon at the church. "If you prayed and believed," she said, "then your prayers would be answered." Still, I knew my prayers must end with "Thy will be done." Maybe God didn't want me to have the doll.

At dawn I awakened with a start. My heart quivered as I slipped from my covers to the iciness of the wooden floor.

At the parlor door my world reeled— **the doll leaned against a shoe box.**

Believing in my child's heart that this was all Santa's doing, I hurried to my parents' bed to show them my treasure. Then I took my doll back to bed with me. There I clutched her to my heart, her beautiful eyes closing in sleep until my father built the fire and we all got up to see our shoes.

From then on the cherished doll transformed my days. Her cloth body yielded to my love as I made her clothes, took her on walks in the sun-warmed pasture, let her soar in the great swing hanging from the oak, showed her new-born piglets and calves tottering on frail legs, and put her to bed at night. On special days I took her to the corn fields where I gave her silken hair from the golden tassels to go on her beautifully shaped head.

To this day I can shut my eyes and see her again under the tree that icy December morning. True, the doll was a material possession that I had coveted with a longing only a child can know. Yet through the

years it has come to mean far more. I know now just how poor my parents were that year, how much sacrifice the doll meant. And today—over forty years later—I know that the miracle of Christmas belongs to those who give.

If my spirit for the Holy Season ever wanes, I gaze at that doll. Her face is cracked; the china blue eyes have faded; the fraying cloth of her body bears darning. Yet to me she is more beautiful then ever. Remembering, my heart prepares itself once more for the precious gift of the Spirit.

In recapturing and reliving my most memorable Christmas, I recall the immortality of my parents' love; love—given and received—the true meaning of Christmas.

THE BLESSING TREE

Norman Vincent Peale

Christmas trees have changed a lot since my boyhood when Father carried a fragrant spruce into the living room. Today one sees all kinds of unusual creations of silver and plastic. But the most unusual one I've heard of is a tree in Florida—a different kind of Christmas tree.

It was put up at the First Methodist Church in Coral Gables one December and caused such a stir that it was never taken down.

The creator, Mrs. Dorothy Culbreath, was meditating one day in early December in the church's Welcome Center room, which serves as a haven for those who wish a moment of quiet, or some fellowship. When the idea came, she and her husband went searching for just the right tree. They saw it—the top part of a lime tree, all covered with black mold—sticking out of a trash pile.

They took it home, cleaned off the mold and sprayed the branches white. When it was transformed into something beautiful, Dorothy and her husband set it up in their church's Welcome Center.

The Sunday bulletin announcement read: "Help us decorate our Blessing Tree. Write on a card the scripture verse which has blessed your life. Then hang it on the tree. Multicolored cards are in the Meditation Room for this purpose." Hundreds were done, and the tree blossomed into beauty.

Members and visitors who needed a spiritual lift went to the tree and found such verses as:

With God all things are possible.
Perfect love casteth out fear.
The Lord knoweth them that trust
    in Him.

Other blessings bloomed on the tree. One woman wrapped six-cent stamps in plastic packets and hung them on the tree with notes saying: "Write someone a cherry note today." Many who took a blessing replaced it with one or more of their own. One member brought a lonely woman she found sitting in the bus station to the church to pick a blessing.

This gave people a chance to be channels for God's love; it was a tree whose fruits brought joy and inspiration to others. As I thought about this unusual tree, I wondered if, perhaps, it weren't the most Christmasy one of them all.